The Leonardo Effect: Motivating Children to Achieve Through Interdisciplinary Learning

'Children learned more in a week than they normally would in a term.'
Fiona Loudon, Head Teacher

'The pupils were captivated by the excitement, a captivation that in turn led to an increase in literacy levels, self-motivation and cooperative learning.'
Emer Vance, Teacher and Scott Vance, Head Teacher

The Leonardo Effect ties together the whole primary curriculum by demonstrating the ways in which art and science can be integrated, allowing children to develop both skills and knowledge. It also equips teachers to teach in a more creative and inspiring manner, improving children's engagement and raising attainment. The method aims to excite children's curiosity and to capture their imaginations, igniting a passion for self-motivated learning.

Divided into two parts, the first section consists of overview chapters written by lecturers in education, including the developers of the methodology, who describe The Leonardo Effect's unique method of integrating art and science in detail, and the outcomes achievable. Part two comprises a series of illustrated case studies contributed by teachers and head teachers who have embedded The Leonardo Effect in their schools, found it has transformed their curriculum, and been positively evaluated by inspectors. These case studies deal with:

- literacy;
- creativity;
- disaffected learners;
- learners with special needs;
- school leadership; and
- assessment.

This book is based on the experiences of researchers, teachers and head teachers who tested The Leonardo Effect in primary schools throughout the British Isles. It has been shown to transform children's learning and raise attainment. Feedback from the schools demonstrates how it enhances teaching and learning.

The Leonardo Effect is ideal for students and practising teachers, curriculum developers and academics working in the field of education.

Ivor Hickey has lectured in science, medicine and education and has published extensively in all three areas.

Deirdre Robson is Head of Art in St Mary's University College and lectures in art with education. Her interest is in creative curriculum design and development, and the importance of artistic expression in children's learning.

The Leonardo Effect: Motivating Children to Achieve Through Interdisciplinary Learning

Edited by Ivor Hickey
and Deirdre Robson

Routledge
Taylor & Francis Group

LONDON AND NEW YORK

First published 2013
by Routledge
2 Park Square, Milton Park, Abingdon, Oxon OX14 4RN

Simultaneously published in the USA and Canada
by Routledge
711 Third Avenue, New York, NY 10017

Routledge is an imprint of the Taylor & Francis Group, an informa business

British Library Cataloguing in Publication Data
A catalogue record for this book is available from the British Library

Library of Congress Cataloging in Publication Data
The Leonardo effect : motivating children to achieve through interdisciplinary learning / [edited by] Ivor Hickey and Deirdre Robson.
p. cm.
Includes bibliographical references and index.
1. Education, Elementary—Curricula—Great Britain. 2. Interdisciplinary approach in education—Great Britain. 3. Motivation in education—Great Britain.
4. Creative teaching—Great Britain. I. Hickey, G. I. (G. Ivor) II. Robson, Deirdre.
LB1564.G7L46 2013
372.190941—dc23
2012022485

ISBN: 978–0–415–60483–3 (hbk)
ISBN: 978–0–415–60484–0 (pbk)
ISBN: 978–0–203–81791–9 (ebk)

Typeset in Bembo
by Swales & Willis Ltd, Exeter, Devon

To teachers across the British Isles who piloted
The Leonardo Effect and found that the road to
achieving pupil potential is paved with curiosity,
creativity and listening to children.

'Do bees ever fly in straight lines?'

Contents

Preface   ix

Foreword   x
   Mick Waters

Acknowledgements   xii

Contributors   xiv

Introduction   1

PART ONE: Overview   9

1 Art Education at the Heart of Learning   11
   Maryann Flanagan

2 The Way Forward for Science Education   24
   Ivor Hickey

3 The Leonardo Effect: Rationale, Methodology and Mechanism   37
   Deirdre Robson

4 The Leonardo Effect: Putting Theory into Practice   51
   Deirdre Robson

**5 Analysis of Feedback from Schools Taking Part in
The Leonardo Effect Pilot   67**
   Ivor Hickey, Deirdre Robson and Maryann Flanagan

**6 Buried Treasure: Uncovering Literacy Jewels in
The Leonardo Effect   83**
   Geraldine Magennis and Paula Campbell

PART TWO: Case Studies   97

  7 **Creativity on Fire in Ynystawe**   99
      Carolyn Davies, Lynne Bebb, Gwenith Davies, Sarah Richards and Rachel Parkes

  8 **Jordanstown School Applies The Leonardo Effect in Teaching with Children who are Deaf or Visually Impaired**   108
      Barbara McGuigan and Gail Lawther

  9 **A Head Teacher Reflects**   115
      Fiona Loudon

 10 **Walking the Earth with our Eyes Turned Skyward**   120
      Emer Vance and Scott Vance

 11 **Synchronised Integration of Art and Science: A Model for Excellence in the Scottish Primary Classroom**   125
      Jem Anderson

 12 **A Student Teacher Asks: Can The Leonardo Effect Enhance Literacy Attainment in Boys?**   132
      Helen McKernan

 13 **Assessment of The Leonardo Effect Learning in Our School**   140
      Dyfrig Ellis

      Conclusion   147

Appendix   149
Glossary   152
Index   153

Preface

Across the world governments are attempting to raise standards in educational achievement. This is seen as an economic and societal imperative. In the drive for improvement, the process of learning is sometimes lost sight of and replaced by assessment. At the same time, the concept of lifelong learning is also championed by governments to meet demands of the rapidly changing global economic world in which we live. Lifelong learning is dependent on the acquisition of skills necessary to gain knowledge, but these are difficult to assess. All too often this results in easily assessed skills such as numeracy and literacy dominating classroom teaching, reducing the role of the child to that of a passive learner, dependent on acquiring facts and techniques provided by the teachers. In our experience this is not how teachers, parents and pupils wish the learning environment to be.

It is in response to this situation that we have developed an approach to teaching that recognises that children have inherent skills conducive to learning and active attitudes towards discovering how their world works. These should be nurtured and capitalised upon. In The Leonardo Effect, children have the freedom to investigate their world utilising their scientific and artistic skills, expressing themselves in the process and developing their potential to innovate. Teachers facilitate the learning, adapting it to relate to children's interests and using their professionalism to guide the direction of the work.

Teachers report that they find this approach invigorating and empowering. It not only allows children's creative abilities to develop, but also enhances knowledge, literacy and numeracy in ways that fulfil governmental wishes, and those of the STEM agenda. The chapters of this book reflect the educational underpinning of the work and also the responses of those who have experienced The Leonardo Effect in practice.

Ivor Hickey and Deirdre Robson

Foreword

It has always seemed odd to me that many people want to separate the study of the arts from the sciences and, in turn, separate them both from other disciplines such as history. To me it is more important to appreciate what they have in common than to worry about the differences that separate them. They are all constructs for our understanding of the way our world has evolved. Each offers a narrative of human discovery with a chronicle of achievement, error and mischief. History, art and science each have examples of contentious impact in their pasts, but they have all contributed to our society in different ways and will continue to do so as we go forward. Each of the disciplines represents change within a defined context and it is foolish to value one above another.

Of course, Leonardo da Vinci did not have the problem of people trying to split him in several ways. He simply learned, wondered, pondered, hypothesised, invented, built and experimented. In short, he gathered knowledge and skills and then, faced with helping others understand, he found ways to explain. He drew, he built, he modelled, he painted, he wrote.

Centuries later, we look at the work of Leonardo and admire his capacity to imagine the future and prompt others to action. We admire his art and his science; we admire his intellect.

This book records the work of teachers who have sought to develop the intellect of the children they teach through a focus on The Leonardo Effect. Integrating the creative with the logical, the experiment with the record, the science with the art and helping children to see the connectedness of learning experiences. True, the children will see the difference and diversities of knowledge-gathering techniques employed by modern-day scientists and they will also appreciate the different process skills of modern-day artists. The specialisms will gradually emerge based on detailed and focused extension of thinking and they will see how seams of science and art run parallel, overlap with each other and with other disciplines and most times form a rich conglomerate of learning to quarry.

Teachers and educationalists across the British Isles have worked on embedding The Leonardo Effect in schools. They have explored possibilities in secondary schools, special schools and in colleges. They have looked at opportunities with parents, experienced and novice teachers, and with learners. They have looked at aspects of learning concerned with assessment, planning, teaching approaches and individual needs. They tell their stories with the humility that makes others think

'I could try that' and in turn become the active knowledge producers in the world of learning and teaching.

The result is a readable, interesting and valuable source of inspiration for those who know it is the right way forward but who are not sure where to start. It is also a spur for those who have taken steps and need to consider where to go next. The case studies point the way, pose questions, describe solutions and sketch out possibilities. They draw us into the complex world of learning in a way that expresses the obvious and the unbelievable side by side.

Enjoy the book. Leonardo would love it.

Professor Mick Waters
University of Wolverhampton

Acknowledgements

The creation of this book is the result of a process that began in 2004 with a small idea sparking research in schools. Accordingly, our heartfelt thanks go to all those in the interim period who have in various ways contributed to making this book a reality.

First of all we owe a debt of gratitude to the schools involved in the early development of the approach and those teachers and head teachers who put faith in our idea. These schools located in Northern Ireland are: Botanic Primary School, Our Lady Queen of Peace Primary School, Silverstream Primary School and St Joseph's Primary School. At this stage the work was known as 'Flights of Imagination: Synchronized Integration of Art and Science in the Primary Curriculum'. We are grateful to ESCalate (Education Subject Centre Advancing Learning and Teaching in Education) who allocated us seed funding at this time accompanied by the prediction that there was more potential in the idea than we realised. Subsequently we were delighted when the Paul Hamlyn Foundation supplemented this funding. We are especially grateful to Shona McCarthy who gave us immense support and valuable advice, Michael Hamlyn and Roger Graef who visited us in Belfast and whose words of encouragement have remained with us.

We are immensely indebted to NESTA (National Endowment for Science Technology and the Arts) who funded The Leonardo Effect pilot in 2007, and in particular we wish to thank Siobhan Edwards and Helen Clare for their expert guidance and sincere belief that our work would make a difference. One post-primary school and 18 primary schools drawn from across the British Isles participated in the pilot and we would like to thank all of the schools, their teachers, head teachers, support staff and school governors for the commitment they gave to sincerely embracing the approach. Only for their professionalism and dedication to collecting data, exhibiting children's work, attending training etc, this book would not exist. These schools are: Ashton Gate Primary School, Avonmouth Primary School, Braidside Integrated Primary School, Carolside Primary School, Cavehill Primary School, Crookfur Primary School, Gaelscoil na Bhfal, Ghyllgrove Community Junior School, Manor Primary School, St Bernard's Primary School, St Malachy's High School, St Peter's Boys National School, Jordanstown School, Knockbreda Primary School, Oakwood School, Star Primary School, St Joseph's Primary School, Ynystawe Primary School and Ysgol Lon Las, thank you.

We are extremely grateful to all of the contributors to this book, who in many other ways as well have been ambassadors for The Leonardo Effect over the last few years. We would like to thank them for their perspectives that have informed our thinking and for the invaluable contribution made in disseminating The Leonardo Effect.

Certain individuals warrant a particular word of thanks. We would like to express our gratitude to Paula Campbell for her excellent work as research officer during the pilot. We sincerely thank Mick Waters for writing the Foreword to the book, for his keynote at the national results launch in 2007 and the time he took to engage in discourse with us. We wish to extend special thanks to our colleague and friend Maryann Flanagan for her input to both pilots and to this book. Her advice and insight have always been greatly valued and appreciated. Our appreciation must also go to Frank Creamer in the Scottish Government for his extended input, communication and support. Thanks to our old friend and colleague Barbara Ellison who made valuable contributions at the inception of the work.

We wish to express our gratitude to Michael Ellis, Dermot Donnelly and Anthony Clearn for their technical help and support especially with preparations for exhibitions etc. and to Paul Conlon for his expertise in respect of photographs and graphic design. We would like to thank Damian Knipe for advice on questionnaires and data analysis.

Thank you to the parents of pupils from St Brendan's Primary School in Craigavon, Ynystawe Primary School in Swansea and Jordanstown School in Newtownabbey who kindly gave permission for us to include photographs of their children.

A very special thank you to our own families and friends for their undying encouragement, love and support during the research and in the creation of the book.

And finally, most important of all we are indebted to the children 'the little Leonardos' whose enthusiasm, joy and excitement for learning in this way inspired and motivated us to write this book and communicate its message to a wider audience.

Contributors

Professor Mick Waters, University of Wolverhampton
Maryann Flanagan, Senior Lecturer, St Mary's University College, Belfast
Ivor Hickey, Principal Lecturer, St Mary's University College, Belfast
Deirdre Robson, Head of Art, St Mary's University College, Belfast
Karen Jones, Vice Principal, Ysgol G.G. Lon Las, Swansea
Geraldine Magennis, Senior Lecturer, St Mary's University College, Belfast
Paula Campbell, Vice Principal, St James's Primary School, Newtownabbey
Carolyn Davies, Education Adviser, Consultant and Arts Practitioner at Oyster Education
Lynne Bebb, Artist
Gwenith Davies, Head Teacher, Ynystawe Primary School, Swansea
Sarah Richards, Teacher, Ynystawe Primary School, Swansea
Rachel Parkes, Teacher, Ynystawe Primary School, Swansea
Barbara McGuigan, Teacher, Jordanstown School, Newtownabbey
Gail Lawther, Teacher, Jordanstown School, Newtownabbey
Fiona Louden, Head Teacher, Crookfur Primary School, East Renfrewshire
Emer Vance, Teacher, St Peter's Boys' National School, Bray, County Wicklow
Scott Vance, Head Teacher, St Peter's Boys' National School, Bray, County Wicklow
Jem Anderson, Teacher, Kirkhill Primary School, Glasgow
Helen McKernan, Student Teacher
Dyfrig Ellis, Head Teacher, Ysgol G.G. Lon Las, Swansea

Introduction

Think of pupils seated in classrooms, each allocated their own small space to work. The *good* pupils listen and respond, complying for five or six hours a day, over nine months of the year. Such a situation is generally regarded as conducive to learning. These children are attentive, well behaved, cooperative, but even with this high level of compliance show only a glimpse of their true potential. The rest of the pupils, well, they are another story!

Similarly, when children are taught and assessed to a narrow range of learning objectives, itemising learning, often in teacher-led lessons, only certain aspects of their potential are revealed or given scope to develop. We believe this practice sets a limit on attainment, depersonalises learning and ultimately damages motivation to learn. It is likely to dominate teaching where quantifiable and commonly measured outcomes are sought and teachers have no autonomy or scope to inspire. We believe this approach only engages with certain facets of those children who conform, and contributes little to motivating or educating the whole child, specifically the great many children who crave involvement in their learning, have a need to express themselves and think independently, and it is in this milieu that they thrive.

Pring and Pollard, in their appraisal of education reviews carried out in the UK between 2006 and 2010, concluded that: 'the Reviews warn against the narrowing of those aims to purely academic achievement or to what is easily measurable. Such narrowness guarantees "educational failure" to many who have achieved much and who demonstrate the benefits of a wider vision of learning' (2011: 17). In our opinion, to teach in a manner that selectively chooses to educate only certain aspects of the child is ill-judged. We believe that children are much more capable than conventional teaching permits. They are born with the attributes of artists and scientists and the desire to learn. They are naturally inquisitive, eager to explore and experiment, to ask questions and to communicate their ideas. To watch children at play should convince anyone of this. They have their own thoughts, motivations and need for independence, even before their verbal communication skills are sufficiently developed to articulate what they are thinking. Children need to move about, engage in singing, dancing and role play, use their imaginations and build their own knowledge from first-hand experience and through making connections. They want to construct things and should have materials available to do so.

The best schools realise this and are striving for involvement of pupils in driving their own learning, despite knowing the demands this places on teachers. They recognise that children have a voice that should be heard. They tend to be creative schools, with head teachers who reflect in depth on their role and the role of education in the lives of all of their pupils. These head teachers are prepared to think independently, be adventurous and engage children in dynamic, innovative, flexible learning situations. They understand the nature of childhood and address all of the needs of the child; understandably their schools achieve highly in inspections.

The Leonardo Effect is a method that teachers can use to engage the diverse range of aptitudes that are found in children, blending these into creative, productive and enjoyable learning experiences. Throughout our work we have met many head teachers who could envisage the application of The Leonardo Effect within their schools and have taken steps to embed it. Several of these inspiring individuals and teachers from their schools have contributed chapters to this book.

Curricular changes

Each region of the UK developed its own 'national curriculum' in the 1980s. This was probably necessary to ensure that there was uniformity of opportunity for children attending state schools. However, it was subsequently realised that these curricula were excessively knowledge based and lacked sufficient opportunity for pupils to develop skills such as creativity. The latter was emphasised in the report, *All Our Futures*, from the National Advisory Committee on Creativity, Culture and Education (NACCCE 1999). NACCCE was set up '[t]o make recommendations to the Secretaries of State on the creative and cultural development of young people through formal and informal education: to take stock of current provision and to make proposals for principles, policies and practice' (NACCCE 1999: 2). Chaired by Sir Ken Robinson and composed of prominent scientists, artists, educators and business leaders, it concluded that creative and cultural education was poorly served by the National Curriculum, and that this affected not only the arts and humanities but also the sciences. The latter is important because creativity is not often associated with science in the minds of the general public. However, considerable efforts have been made to support the teaching of creativity in the sciences. This is evidenced by the number of books published on creativity in science education and editions of the Association for Science Education's (ASE) journals *Primary Science* and *School Science Review* themed on creativity in science.

Revisions made to curricula in Northern Ireland, Scotland and Wales have attempted to achieve a balance between conceptual knowledge and transferable skills. As a result, much more prominence has been given to thinking skills, organisation of knowledge and education of children to become confident contributors to society. In Scotland, *Curriculum for Excellence* (Scottish Government 2004) has stressed the value of interdisciplinary learning. It has been taken up in Local Education Authorities, for example:

> All primary schools include interdisciplinary learning across the school ensuring a strong and challenging focus on subject knowledge and understanding. Some primary schools have used the Leonardo Effect. This is a teaching methodology that integrates subjects and develops pupils' skills. It allows pupils to deepen their understanding of existing knowledge and skills and develop new learning in Science and Art . . . Knowledge and skills in art and science greatly exceeded age-appropriate norms for many children.
>
> (East Dunbarton Education Service 2011)

In addition, considerable weight has been placed on the learning of subjects in a meaningful context. The Northern Ireland Curriculum (CCEA 2006) has grouped traditional subjects such as geography, history and science into a single learning area entitled the World Around Us, with an emphasis on studying topics in a broader contextual setting. The new English curriculum will not be implemented until 2014, but is likely to be influenced by reports such as *The Cambridge Primary Review*:

> It asks the fundamental question 'What is primary education for?' and answered it with a list of aims which reflect values and should drive the curriculum. Those values arise from what it means to become 'an educated person', namely, developing the capacities in young children:
>
> ■ to make sense of their experiences and thereby be empowered through knowledge;
>
> ■ to have a sense of personal fulfilment; to be actively engaged in their learning;
>
> ■ to have moral qualities of respect and caring;
>
> ■ to participate actively in the wider group in anticipation of becoming active citizens.
>
> (cited by Pring and Pollard 2011: 15)

This broader view on the role of education in children's lives is a philosophy we subscribe to.

Art and science

The idea to bring art and science together in children's learning, as we do in The Leonardo Effect, is not new. Readers may be familiar with C.P. Snow's Rede lecture of 1959 'The Two Cultures and the Scientific Revolution'. Snow identified a gulf created by separation. He saw it as a barrier to our creative thinking and achievements. He believed that educational systems, from schools through to universities, needed to change (Snow 2003). Bronowski (1978) also emphasised the need to develop the full potential of mankind, and believed that to do so collaboration between the literary/visual/musical arts and sciences was essential. Similar comments have been raised more recently by the chairman of Google, Dr Eric Schmidt. This topic is explored in more depth in Chapter 3.

At its most basic level, interdisciplinary learning involving art and science enables pupils to take more than one perspective on a problem, to be armed with experience and knowledge and therefore be better prepared to solve it. On a practical level, it makes learning more appealing by providing multiple access points corresponding with children's range of aptitudes. It also sets learning in real-world contexts, giving relevance and meaning. At its most meaningful, given space and time, it provides the opportunity for informed exploration, creativity and eureka moments. It is in this realm that innovation happens. As Wilson says 'The future will be enriched if this expansion of zones of interest becomes a part of the definition of art and science' (2003: 3).

We are edging towards Snow's vision; for example, on The Art of Science Learning website Harvey Seifter comments that:

> Responding to concerns that the U.S. risks lagging behind other nations [. . .] in both the scientific literacy and the innovative capacity of its workforce, the Art of Science Learning convened scientists, artists, educators, business leaders, researchers and policymakers in three conferences in Spring 2011 to explore how the arts can be engaged to strengthen STEM skills and spark creativity in the 21st-Century American workforce.
>
> (The Art of Science Learning 2012: np)

Fifty years after Snow, a new paradigm is gradually emerging – one where creativity, innovation and interdisciplinarity focusing particularly on the arts and sciences is being explored. In April 2012 OECD/CERI presented the findings of their report on the role of arts education in developing skills for innovation-driven societies (OECD 2012). Le Laboratoire's network of art science labs on several continents is working with university undergraduates and high-school students. However, apart from our own work in developing The Leonardo Effect, we can find little evidence of art science interaction at the level of school curricula. Modernisation of school curricula could be described as falling behind.

STEM to STEAM

Since embarking on developing The Leonardo Effect, STEM education (science, technology, engineering and mathematics) has come to prominence and been funded on a massive scale globally. The promise of STEM to enable pupils to transfer and use knowledge across the disciplines, inspire innovation and contribute to the economy is a powerful incentive to governments. We however subscribe to the STEM to STEAM movement, which aims to put art and design into STEM. This view is spreading, for example, through developments such as STEAM (www. steam-notstem.com), ARTStem at the University of North Carolina School of the Arts (www.artstem.org) and Stem to Steam at Rhode Island School of Design (www.stemtosteam.org), where the president John Maeda explains:

> When policymakers today talk about education and reform, it's all about the STEM subjects. It's about convergent thinking – problem solving by breaking it down. Instead, a divergent thinker takes an idea and looks to expand it, and to find new diverse ways to connect it [. . .] You need both to create balance: combining STEM with the Arts to get STEAM. In the past 20 years, we've focused too much on technology innovation. Art and design humanize those developments, and fuel true innovation, which ultimately leads to economic recovery and leadership.
>
> (Maeda 2011: np)

Support for the transition from STEM to STEAM is increasingly voiced by UK Culture Minister Ed Vasey and UK Science Minister David Willetts. David Willetts recently stated 'instead of just thinking about STEM, Science, Technology, Engineering and Maths, we should add the Arts so it becomes STEAM' (Cabinet Office 2012: np).

The Leonardo Effect has already put the 'A' into STEM. The outcomes are dramatic, and demonstrate the asset of creative thinking though art in increasing learning attainment. The Leonardo Effect inspires and motivates children to learn, innovate and achieve success beyond everyone's expectations. We emphasise how important it is to ensure that the integrity of the individual disciplines is retained, and part of this process requires the subject hierarchy that has developed in western education in the last 100 years to be dissolved.

The Leonardo Effect in brief

In support of an art science symbiosis, the late physicist David Bohm believed that it was adults who created the unnatural separation between art and science, which children did not. He said, 'they [children] are gradually trained to think, feel, and perceive in terms of this kind of separation' (Bohm 1998: 80).

Our methodology, synchronised integration of art and science, was first tested with art and science via a preliminary study conducted in the greater Belfast area during 2004–2005, entitled 'Flights of Imagination: Synchronised Integration of Art and Science in the Primary Curriculum'. The research was funded by the Paul Hamlyn Foundation and ESCalate. NESTA subsequently funded a pilot of the approach involving each of the curricular regions of the British Isles during 2006–2007, under the title 'The Leonardo Effect: Synchronised Integration of Art and Science in the Curriculum'. The externally evaluated pilot involved approximately 1,100 pupils from 18 primary schools and 179 pupils from a single large secondary school. Since completion of the pilot, the number of primary schools using the approach has steadily increased. A further pilot at post-primary level funded by The Esmée Fairbairn Foundation is currently approaching completion.

Chapter synopses

The book is presented in two parts. The first consists of six chapters that explore the theoretical background to The Leonardo Effect and the data obtained from our pilot in primary schools. The second part concentrates on case studies exploring aspects of The Leonardo Effect in schools, authored by head teachers and teachers.

The first chapter, entitled 'Art Education at the Heart of Learning', is written by Maryann Flanagan, a senior lecturer in fine art and art education in Northern Ireland. She reflects on issues about current art teaching in primary school against an examination of the nature of the subject, and proposes a rethinking of the role of art in education. The companion to this is Chapter 2, where Ivor Hickey outlines 'The Way Forward for Science Education'. Science education has been intensively studied during the last decade, because of the perceived need for more science graduates. He discusses the main arguments in the development of science curricula that have moved significantly towards embracing the concept of scientific literacy. In Chapter 3, 'The Leonardo Effect: Rationale, Methodology and Mechanism', Deirdre Robson presents the academic foundation underpinning Synchronised Integration of Art and Science, also known as The Leonardo Effect. The structure of the model and the mechanism that enables teachers to apply it in schools is explained and justified. In Chapter 4, entitled 'The Leonardo Effect: Putting Theory into Practice', she explains how to carry the theory of The Leonardo Effect into practice. This is supported by examples of teaching from Karen Jones, a vice-principal who participated in the original pilot. Included also are excerpts from the external evaluation of The Leonardo Effect pilot that was conducted by the TERU unit in Goldsmiths College, University of London. In Chapter 5, Ivor Hickey, Deirdre Robson and Maryann Flanagan present an analysis of the feedback generated by the schools involved in the original NESTA-funded Leonardo Effect pilot. Views of head teachers, teachers, parents and children are included here. Chapter 6, 'Buried Treasure: Uncovering Literacy Jewels in The Leonardo Effect', is written by Geraldine Magennis, senior lecturer in literacy and education in St Mary's University College, Belfast, and Paula Campbell, who was the research officer on the pilot and is now a primary school vice-principal. They reflect on their observations of how literacy outcomes exceeded all expectations and set this in the context of literacy research, guidance and child development.

The second part of the book opens with 'Creativity on Fire in Ynystawe' by Carolyn Davies et al. Ynystawe Primary School in Wales is a thriving creative learning environment and through the eyes of an LEA advisor, artist, the head teacher and teachers, the chapter outlines how The Leonardo Effect was adopted in the school, and used to foster creativity, with praise from HMI inspection. In Chapter 8, Barbara McGuigan, a teacher of the deaf, and Gail Lawther, a teacher of visually impaired children in Jordanstown School, Northern Ireland, speak of how naturally The Leonardo Effect fitted in with their children's needs and their school's philosophy. Chapter 9, 'A Head Teacher Reflects', is written by Fiona Loudon, head teacher in Crookfur Primary School in Scotland. It recounts the impact of her school's involvement in The Leonardo Effect from the perspective of pupils and parents, the experience of an HMIE inspection during implementation of The Leonardo Effect pilot and the legacy the teaching methodology has had in her school.

In Chapter 10, 'Walking the Earth With Our Eyes Turned Skyward', Emer Vance and Scott Vance discuss The Leonardo Effect being implemented in St Peter's Boys National School in an area of social disadvantage in the Republic of Ireland. Pupils' motivation to lead their own learning, behaviour modification, pupils' desire to read in order to find answers to their own questions and greater parental involvement are just a few of the aspects explored in context. In Chapter 11, Jem Anderson describes how she embraced the methodology as a newly qualified teacher and then went on to adopt the methodology in her general practice, including working with Primary 1 children. She reflects on how it accomplishes the requirements of a Curriculum for Excellence (2007) in Scotland and recommends it as a model for all.

In Chapter 12, 'A Student Teacher Asks: Can The Leonardo Effect Enhance Literacy Attainment in Boys?,' Helen McKernan, a student teacher in her final teaching placement, chose to explore The Leonardo Effect's potential for engaging boys and improving their literacy attainment. She was motivated by the need in this area and the suspicion that The Leonardo Effect had the potential to make a strong impact. She found that this was indeed the case. In the final chapter, Dyfrig Ellis head teacher in Ysgol Lon Las in Wales, confronts the challenging area of assessment of skills. The Leonardo Effect is now fully embedded in his school and teachers use an online assessment tool that ensures children's full range of skills are accurately recorded and relayed to parents. The school came through inspection in December 2012 with an excellent rating and this is discussed as part of the chapter.

References

Bohm, D. (1998) in L. Nichol, *On Creativity*, London: Routledge.

Bronowski, J. (1978) *The Visionary Eye: Essays in the arts, literature and science*, Cambridge, MA: The MIT Press.

Cabinet Office (2012) *David Willetts' Speech – Our hi-tech future – Policy Exchange, Westminster*. Online. Available at: http://www.culture.gov.uk/news/ministers_speeches/8853.aspx (accessed 6 May 2012).

CCEA (2006) The Northern Ireland Curriculum. Online. Available at: http://www.nicurriculum.org.uk (accessed 5 May 2012).

East Dunbarton Education Service (2011) Standards and Quality Report 2010/2011.

Online. Available at: http://www.eastdunbarton.gov.uk/pdf/Education%20Qlty %20Improve/ED%20-%20QI%20EDC%20Education%20Service%20Standards%2 0&%20Quality%20Report%202010-2011.pdf (accessed 24 April 2012).

Maeda, J. (2011) *Bridging STEM to STEAM: Developing new frameworks for art-science-design pedagogy*. Online. Available at: http://www.risd.edu/templates/content. aspx?id=4294974805 (accessed 6 May 2012).

National Advisory Committee on Creative and Cultural Education. NACCCE (1999) *All Our Futures: Creativity, culture and education*, London: DFEE.

OECD (2012) Educating for Innovative Societies, Conference 26 April 2012, Paris, France. Online. Available at: http://www.oecd.org/document/15/0,3746,en_ 21571361_49995565_49798543_1_1_1_1,00.html (accessed 24 April 2012).

Pring, R. and Pollard, A. (2011) *Education for All: Evidence from the past, principles for the future*. Online. Available at: http://www.tlrp.org/educationforall/EducationForAll. pdf (accessed 6 May 2012).

Scottish Government (2007) *A Curriculum for Excellence*. Online. Available at: http://www. educationscotland.gov.uk/thecurriculum/index.asp (accessed 30 July 2012).

Snow, C.P. (2003) *The Two Cultures*, Reprint, Cambridge: Cambridge University Press.

The Art of Science Learning (2012) Shaping the 21st-Century Workforce. Online. Available at: http://www.artofsciencelearning.org (accessed 10 May 2012).

Wilson, S. (2003) *Information Arts: Intersections of art, science and technology*, London: The MIT Press.

Overview

1

Art Education at the Heart of Learning

Maryann Flanagan

This chapter will present the opportunities that exist in education today for art to play an instrumental role in children's learning and development, against a backdrop of the traditionally peripheral role it has occupied. The reasons for this are explored and a 21st-century vision is presented.

'Art is part of the human condition' (Barnes 2001: 7). This is evident even in very young children who relish mark-making, not just with standard art tools, but in spilt food, on steamed-up windows or in wet sand, even before the development of spoken language, and certainly before the acquisition of reading and writing skills. The desire or need to communicate and express visually continues into adulthood across all cultures, and is evidenced by galleries and museums around the globe, pointing to 'a fundamental need in us to make visual expression of who and what we are' (Barnes 2001: 7). But how is this basic and deep-seated human instinct acknowledged and developed in primary school education?

Drawing Together: Art, Craft and Design in Schools (Ofsted 2009) evaluated the strengths and weaknesses of art, craft and design in a sample of primary and secondary schools in England. It found that while standards in art and design in primary schools were good in one-third of the schools inspected, in the other two-thirds 'some work was of good quality but standards and provision were too variable' (Ofsted 2009: 4). Although it may be unclear how standards were judged or what constitutes 'good quality' artwork in primary schools, it is worth noting that '[many] pupils had only a limited understanding of the subject and its importance' (2009: 4). This notion has been upheld recently in the *Cambridge Primary Review*, which reported that 'Some [contributors] felt that, generally speaking, art was not well handled in the primary curriculum' (Alexander 2010: 227).

Similar findings have been reported in other countries. In the USA, The President's Committee on the Arts and the Humanities (PCAH) began its 2011 report by stressing that education in the arts is more important than ever. However, the report goes on to illustrate a decline in the provision of meaningful access to the arts for children (2011: 30), despite numerous studies indicating the benefits of arts education in 'producing better attendance and fewer discipline problems, increased graduation rates, and improved test scores; motivating students who were difficult to reach otherwise; and providing challenges to more academically successful students' (2011: 19).

Challenges within art education

What are the challenges facing art education in the 21st century? When finances are under pressure, or time is short, it is invariably art, music or drama that is axed. Moreover, increasing emphasis on literacy and numeracy has pushed the arts further down the list of priorities for primary school teachers and 'the status of the subject has been reduced by lack of attention and diversion of resources' (Herne 2009: 122). In addition to this, the nature and role of art in primary education is widely misunderstood. Consequences resulting from this misunderstanding are highlighted here. It is imperative that we begin to address the situation by eliciting the true nature of art and putting forward the case for raising its profile in primary school education.

Firstly, there is a cyclical impact within a school context, leading to poor and ineffective practice. This results in a devaluation of the subject, and generates indifference and disregard among school staff, parents and indeed the pupils, thereby perpetuating the misunderstanding. If the nature and role of art in primary education are not fully appreciated, the legitimacy and worth of art activities taking place in the classroom can be dubious at best. When art is not grounded in or does not involve genuine learning experiences, it can be regarded as inessential, useful merely in creating an attractive learning environment, but not important in the business of the school and superfluous to the education of children. Art, in this scenario, is understandably not valued.

Art in primary school is sometimes simply regarded as decoration, and art lessons are used to create displays. Often teachers plan their art lessons with the intention of covering a display board; neither children's learning nor their development feature in the planning or preparation. Although it is very important to create a stimulating learning environment that includes prominent display of children's art, a problem occurs when art is produced solely for display. Not only does learning take a backseat in such a situation, but because the purpose is to decorate the classroom, teachers take ownership of the activity. This can mean that neatness, order, symmetry and uniformity are used as criteria for assessing the suitability of the work for display, representing an adult's rather than a child's perspective on the artwork. Tragically, where teachers neither appreciate children's artistic efforts nor value the learning involved, the end result is often the use of templates or colouring-in activities in the name of art.

A second effect of this misunderstanding is teachers' lack of confidence in both their own artistic ability and their competence teaching art. 'I'm no good at art, I can't teach it' is an expression that is often heard. If it is accepted that teaching art requires the teacher to have the 'arty' ideas, then naturally the teacher will assess his or her own artistic talent and capability to do so. I would strenuously argue that teachers do not need to be technically skilful at art in order to teach the subject effectively in the primary school.

A further manifestation of the failure to acknowledge the value of art in the learning and development of children is found when art is offered as a treat for good behaviour on Friday afternoon, or withheld as punishment for misbehaviour. The implicit message to the children is that art is not important; it is a disposable part of the timetable and it is therefore not really about learning or education. We are saying to children that their artwork is not valued, that art is not a serious activity and that children who show talent or interest in art are not as important as those who excel in other areas of the curriculum. What provision is made for children in our classrooms whose talents, passion and future lie in art?

Art is very often delivered in primary schools as an add-on, where it is simply attached to lessons and used to illustrate learning in other curricular areas. Drawing pictures of characters from literature or making Neolithic houses in history is less concerned with learning in art and more about giving children an enjoyable interlude in a topic being covered elsewhere. Generally speaking, this type of activity in the primary classroom pays only lip service to art education. Art, like all subjects and learning areas of the primary curriculum should first and foremost be about children's learning and development. The starting point in the planning of any lesson is to identify the learning that the pupils should achieve. Why should planning for art be any different?

It seems that the only way to change these erroneous perceptions of primary art education, which result in many of our children being short-changed by missing out on an intrinsic element of their education, is to identify the fundamental principles of successful art education in the primary school.

The nature of art

In order to gain an understanding of education in art, we must first consider the nature of art itself. It is of course extremely difficult to define art in any emphatic or succinct way, and I do not intend to espouse any new theoretical points of view, but simply accept that art is a 'multifaceted, complex and contested phenomenon' (Hickman 2010: 7). Consideration of this may shed light on the discussion of art in education and inform our perspective. Some argue that art and any explanations of it are subjective, while others highlight the ever-changing nature of the discipline and insist that it is the developmental, progressive and even controversial aspects of art that define it. In light of possible ambiguity, and for the purposes of this chapter, it is useful to focus on the way artists work, the processes, procedures and methods they employ throughout their creative journey, from the initial inception of ideas, through to the final realisation of artwork. Artists progress through a series of common stages, whether working on a fine art piece such as a painting, sculpture, installation, video or conceptual piece; or a work of design, in areas such as textiles, fashion, graphics, furniture or architecture. In order to get the most from ideas and to ensure the optimum development after the initial motivation, artists carry out research and gather an array of information; they explore and experiment; they develop their ideas; and they engage in critical reflection and creation. This has major relevance for teaching and learning experiences in primary school art; Hetland et al. draw an interesting and valuable parallel with teaching and learning in mathematics, science, history and linguistics to point out that children should be given the opportunity to 'think like artists' (2007: 4).

Accepting this view of the processes of art, what are the implications for art education, and in particular teaching art in the primary school, and what does this mean for the primary school teacher? To answer these questions it is necessary to consider:

- the characteristics of valid artistic learning experiences;

- the role of the teacher in the learning processes of art;

- the part that the child plays in his or her artistic learning and development; and

- the learning context.

Learning in art

How we view the nature of learning in art is fundamental to how we teach the subject. Effective teaching in art and design reflects a situated perspective of learning, where the very nature of the subject is aligned with a socio-cultural view of mind. The artist, including the child artist, is always active or agentive in the creative process and invariably learns from mistakes and from finding solutions to problems and dilemmas that arise naturally as part of the creative process. It seems reasonable to conclude that learning in art therefore is synonymous with engagement in practical activity. Facilitating and enabling progressive learning in art depends on an emphasis being directed on the processes, experiences and opportunities provided for the children. An example of good practice in this area is shown in Figure 1.1. This enables them to explore the visual elements, experiment with materials, tools and processes, and to investigate and respond to sensory experiences of the world around them. Unfortunately, it could be argued that much classroom practice in primary school art and design reflects a product-oriented approach, which features adults directing children through a series of actions to achieve a pre-designed outcome. Furthermore, this results in assessment that focuses on an adult's perspective on the success of the final product without consideration given to learning processes, the child's intentions and ideas or his or her reflection and evaluation.

Conversely, through valuable and valid art experiences, children learn how to look and see, and to understand what they are looking at. Engagement with art

FIGURE 1.1 Drawing in space: exploring line in three dimensions (Photo: Paul Conlon)

teaches about the visual and tactile elements; how to appreciate and use colour, pattern, shape, space, line, tone and texture. In addition to aesthetic awareness and understanding, important skills using materials, tools and processes are developed. Learning in art is also promoted through opportunities to respond to artworks, although Hickman (2010: 57) maintains that recent emphasis on a subject-centred approach to art education has seen this aspect take prominence, to the detriment of actual art making. He argues for a return to a learner-centred approach and a re-focus on art making if there is to be development in acquiring, developing and refining practical studio skills (2010: 144). It is imperative for children's learning that we have an effective art curriculum that is relevant, contemporary and is not based on outdated notions of art education. Pupils should have access to contemporary art as well as the 'old masters'. My experience indicates that children respond very positively to conceptual and abstract art; it is often teachers and other adults who are reluctant to engage with it. A contemporary art gallery provides children with a stimulating and challenging context for the development of analytical and critical thinking skills, concept formation and communication and perceptual and aesthetic awareness.

This century is perhaps the most visually stimulating ever. We are constantly absorbing imagery via advertisements, movies, websites, video games, music videos and product packaging; we encounter these in an increasing range of immediate and powerful contexts such as television, personal computers, mobile telephones, cinemas and billboards. Children must develop an understanding and appreciation of their visual experiences. They need to learn how to read, interpret and respond to the abundance of literal, symbolic and abstract imagery, which they encounter as part of everyday life in the 21st century. Eisner highlighted this aspect of art education as 'helping students become astute readers of visual images and sensitive, politically informed interpreters of their meanings' (2002: 30). Freedman succinctly defines it as 'visual culture' (2003: 11).

The roles of teacher and learner

It seems clear that some rethinking of the teacher's role in primary school art and design is urgently needed. In the past there has been much discussion about rather extreme approaches to art education, such as a laissez-faire approach, which advocates giving pupils free rein over what they do in art and how they do it without any teacher involvement. On the other hand, the role of the teacher is often misinterpreted as just an instructor or demonstrator, that is, one who shows the children how it should be done, for example how to draw a tree, or make a model of a figure. As well as the danger of this resulting in art lessons that are overly teacher-directed, it puts teachers who lack confidence in their own artistic ability in an extremely uncomfortable position. As already noted, in order to teach art effectively, teachers do not need to be skilled drawers or gifted painters, sculptors, ceramicists or designers; they do however, need to understand the art processes; be familiar with art tools and materials; have curious and inquiring minds and have the professional ability to inspire this in children. They should give children the opportunity to work like artists; to follow the same processes, to develop their ideas, as well as honing techniques and skills. The role of the teacher in developing and promoting learning in art in the primary school includes:

- fostering a classroom ethos that encourages creativity;
- providing access to stimulating sensory experiences;
- encouraging and providing reasons for engagement with these experiences;
- focusing children's observation;

- enabling them to explore their world;

- providing opportunities for experimentation with art materials, tools and processes;

- encouraging on-going reflection and evaluation to inform their development.

Teachers must strive to develop their own creativity, and to offer meaningful and considered creative learning experiences for their pupils. Through the operation of a teaching cycle that involves listening, observing, participating, documenting, reflecting and revisiting, teachers can ensure that children are continually motivated and that artistic learning and creative development are progressive and continuous. It is crucial that teachers support, rather than lead, the creative endeavours of the pupils to enable progression, and ensure that every opportunity for creative expression is afforded to children. However, this is not always the case. The *Cambridge Primary Review* stated 'submissions to the Review united in complaining that children's opportunities to express themselves creatively have been seriously eroded in the past 20 years' (Alexander 2010: 99).

Key tools for teachers in facilitating learning in art and nurturing creative development are interaction, collaboration and engagement. Relationships are crucial in the learning process, and consideration should be given to both symmetric and asymmetric interactions in the classroom. The adult–child, or asymmetric, relationship is regarded as fundamental to successful learning and development; Moran states that 'children and adults socially construct knowledge and create *shared meaning* as they actively engage in activities' (1998: 408). Vygotsky argued that human beings, even the youngest infants, are comprehensively social organisms, and it is only through interaction with others that young children begin to develop a sense of self. Furthermore, development according to Vygotsky proceeds from the social to the individual. The significance of this for art education cannot be ignored. To maximise the learning potential and cultivate pupils' artistic aptitudes, the teacher's role should involve collaborating with pupils, working and learning alongside them, listening to their ideas, theories and desires and making decisions with them, not for them. Fleming observes that 'good teaching requires subtle judgement and sensitivity to context, knowing when it is appropriate, for example, to engage, demonstrate, explain, exemplify, challenge, coax, direct, instruct or stay quiet' (2012: 114).

Kindler and Darras (1997: 20) present a socio–cultural model of artistic development that highlights the place of social interaction in artistic learning. This, they argue, is based on the assumption that all art 'shares communication potential' (1997: 19). From a social–constructivist perspective, the role of the child in the learning activity is as a researcher and as an active constructor of knowledge in collaboration with others. Encouraging children to think like artists and to think of themselves as artists is consistent with a social constructivist approach to learning and is exemplified fully in the Reggio Emilia approach to Early Years' education. As well as this, a key principle of the Reggio Emilia philosophy is that emphasis is placed on teachers simply listening to the children. Teachers can offer support and guidance that enables children to observe with sensitivity; to express their feelings, emotions and ideas; and to communicate using the visual elements. However, children also learn from each other (through symmetric interactions) and they should be provided with opportunities to collaborate at all stages of the art-making process. An example of such an activity is shown in Figure 1.2. Edwards et al. state that in Reggio Emilia, 'Classrooms are organized to support a highly collaborative problem-solving approach to learning' (1998: 7).

This child–centred or child-led approach is consistent with the characteristics of valid learning experiences in art discussed earlier in this chapter, as learning develops out of the pupils' curiosity and interest. Such an approach to education is developmental and 'fosters individual differences and encourages expression and heuristic learning' (Hickman 2010: 135). Furthermore, this approach has at its core a respect for the rights and perspectives of the child; in other words, 'respect for the subjectivity of the learner' (Gandini and Kaminsky 2005: 124).

Learning context

The learning environment provided by the teacher plays a significant role in ensuring that children gain most from the artistic learning experiences offered. This means giving due consideration to, in the first instance, the physical context.

FIGURE 1.2 Investigating new ideas and learning together (Photo: Paul Conlon)

It is important that the pupils have room to move about, and have easy access to materials. They need to have space to work individually and in groups, and room to leave their work and return to it later; it is unrealistic to expect any artist, including the child artist, to complete an investigation or experiment on the first attempt.

The classroom is the main setting for the business of learning, so it is imperative that the intellectual context is a priority for the teacher. In art as in all learning areas, the pupils must be challenged to operate at progressively higher standards. In art this means not just learning new techniques and practical skills, but encouraging progressive creative and critical thinking skills and introducing more complex topics and concepts for inquiry.

The emotional context cannot be left to chance. In order to be creative and engage in the artistic processes, pupils need to be sure of the security and encouragement offered to them by adults. They need to know that they can try something to see if it works and that it is alright if it does not. It is important that they receive encouragement and respect for attempting, succeeding *and* failing, and that they feel their investigations and experiments are valued; they should also be given the time to reflect on them and talk about them if they want to. Within such a supportive environment children will develop empathy and understanding, and learn to value and respect each other's ideas and work. Gradually, in this supportive and structured context, they will develop the skills and confidence to take control of their own artistic learning and direct their own creative development.

Learning through art

Most teachers would recognise that children enjoy art; they love to make and build things, to explore, investigate and create. 'Many children said that they liked subjects where they could use their imagination – art, music, creative writing and drama were all mentioned – and they also valued those subjects that sparked their curiosity and encouraged them to explore' (Alexander 2010: 213). Huge potential exists for teachers to exploit children's enjoyment of art and creative activities as well as their natural curiosity, to engage them in learning. Eisner proposes that we 'turn topsy-turvy the more typical view that the arts are basically sources of relief, ornamental activities intended to play second fiddle to the core processes of education' to consider 'what education can learn from the arts' (2002: 196). He highlights a range of issues and consequences of effective art education that he feels could be employed to good use in education generally. For instance, in art, there is no single correct solution to a problem, and children's individuality and personal interpretations are highly valued. This, he argues, is an attitude that could and indeed should permeate more readily throughout the curriculum, while acknowledging that there are, of course, occasions when it is necessary to arrive at the standard answer. Effective learning and teaching in art encompasses the development of a range of transferable skills in meaningful contexts; these include creativity, problem-solving skills, collaborative skills, managing information, ICT skills, decision making, analytical skills and peer and self-evaluation; in addition, it affords stimulating opportunities to cultivate intellectual, emotional and aesthetic growth in children. Regular engagement with art in an education setting cultivates 'independently sustainable dispositions to life-long learning' (Bell 2011: 42).

'Art educators have long known that art helps students understand the human condition through their investigations of themselves, particularly when they find their own strengths and are allowed to develop them in depth' (Freedman 2008: 345). However, is it feasible to consider art as a medium for learning? If so, is there a danger of diluting learning *in* art, in an effort to promote learning *through* art? There are differing views on this; Hetland et al. strongly believe that 'Arts educators cannot allow the arts to be justified wholly or primarily in terms of what the arts can do for mathematics or reading. The arts must stand on what they teach directly' (2007: 3). Indeed Eisner supports this perspective and postures that 'art education should give pride of place to what is distinctive about the arts. Art education should not get side-tracked or attempt to justify its primary education mission by focussing its efforts on outcomes that other fields can claim to serve equally well' (2002: 42). It is important not to lose sight of the important and fundamental place of art in education, and to recognise the rationale for children's rights to engage in, and learn from, appropriate art experiences throughout their schooling. The *Road Map for Arts Education* (UNESCO 2006) supports the rightful place of arts subjects as discrete and important areas of learning for all children, while at the same time recognising the valuable role of the same arts subjects in an interdisciplinary approach to learning and teaching. Two approaches to arts education are highlighted: '(1) [The arts] taught as individual study subjects, through the teaching of the various arts disciplines, thereby developing students' artistic skills, sensitivity, and appreciation of the arts, (2) [The arts] seen as a method of teaching and learning in which artistic and cultural dimensions are included in all curriculum subjects' (2006: 8). While considering the role of art and design in citizenship education, Hickman (2003: 85) clarifies an important distinction between these two approaches, explaining that the 'emphasis in education through art and design is on education rather than on art and design: the focus being learning about and making art and design as a way of becoming an educated citizen rather than becoming an artist or designer.' While continuing to respect the place of art in education and acknowledge it as important in its own right, there is also a valuable opportunity to take advantage of children's natural enjoyment of it and the characteristics inherent to it that engage pupils and foster learning and development in general.

Fleming discusses the problems inherent in strategies designed to increase attainment in literacy without considering 'the role played by learner motivation' (2012: 112). Participation in art provides stimulating, meaningful and enjoyable contexts for the development of language and literacy skills; conversely, oral language is very important in promoting learning and development in art and is embedded in all stages of the creative processes. Effective questioning by the teacher focuses children's attention on the visual and tactile elements (colour, line, tone, shape, space, pattern and texture) and they should be encouraged to reflect on the specific qualities of these and compare and describe them. Participating in art affords teachers and pupils the chance to explain, describe, instruct, discuss, plan, speculate, question, inform, use descriptive language, recall experiences, share ideas and feelings, listen to each other, ask questions, predict outcomes of experiments, gather and record information in various forms including written. These skills are not specific to art but embrace the whole spectrum of educational development. For example, observing, investigating and recording the natural and man-made environments provides a natural synthesis for learning in areas of science and geography with art. However, science in particular shares several categories of commonality with art.

Although it may be surprising to the casual observer, certain areas of the art and design curriculum overlap strongly with numeracy. Knowledge and understanding of mathematical concepts such as designing and drawing patterns; investigating and talking about pattern in the environment; investigating scale; exploring shape and space; using two-dimensional shapes; exploring and talking about shapes in the environment; discussing the properties of three-dimensional shapes; making models in three dimensions; exploring the properties of a range of materials and sorting collections of materials, can be developed through a broad, balanced and progressive art curriculum.

Conclusion

This chapter began by describing some of the challenges surrounding art education and reflecting on the practical out-workings of these in the classroom. By considering the true nature of art practice and reflecting on the implications for teaching art in the primary school, the importance of art in the education of children was demonstrated, and the key tools discussed. A pedagogy that emphasises active participation, enables pupils to work and think like artists, and that stresses learning and development as central to effective and legitimate art education was proposed. Consideration of art as a medium for learning highlighted some salient points. Clearly there are many opportunities for developing interdisciplinary approaches to education in the primary school that exploit the commonalities that art shares with curricular areas such as those highlighted above; and there are many advantages to be gained from exploiting the nature of art as a conduit for learning and development. Learning through art can be aligned with 'either child-centred, progressive approaches where the focus is more on the personal growth of the individual or, in its more contemporary manifestation, it refers to the use of the arts to promote creative learning in other subjects' (Fleming 2012: 72). The President's Committee on the Arts and Humanities report references evidence from empirical research that documents the benefits of arts integration and is unequivocal in stating that 'the greatest gains in schools with arts integration are often seen school-wide and also with the most hard-to-reach and economically disadvantaged students' (2011: 19).

In his keynote address at the Second World Conference on Arts Education in Seoul, Jean-Pierre Guingané asserted that arts education is a means to develop one's sensibility, emotional intelligence, perception about others, capacity for comparative analysis and understanding towards diversity. He argued that the arts are a tool to (i) express, (ii) explore one's self and surrounding and (iii) reflect deeply. He stated that arts education has the potential to counter the negative impact of globalisation, with its cultural homogenisation, by nurturing creative individuals with their own sense of identity (O'Farrell 2010: 4). Most art educators would surely agree with this vision. The challenge lies in convincing others, taking these ideals forward and realising our vision for 21st-century art education. However, we should take confidence from the encouragement and support offered in the *Cambridge Primary Review*: 'we would wish to encourage a vigorous campaign aimed at advancing public understanding of the arts in education, human development, culture and national life, coupled with a much more rigorous approach to arts teaching in schools. The renaissance of this domain is long overdue' (Alexander 2010: 267).

References

Alexander, R.J. (ed.) (2010) *Children, their World, their Education. Final report and recommendations of the Cambridge Primary Review*, London: Routledge.

Barnes, R. (2001) *Teaching Art to Young Children, 4–11*, London: Routledge Falmer.

Bell, D. (2011) 'Seven ways to talk about art: One conversation and seven questions for talking about art in early childhood settings', *International Journal of Education through Art* 7, 41–54.

Edwards, C., Gandini, L. and Forman, G. (eds) (1998) *The Hundred Languages of Children*, London: Ablex.

Eisner, W.E. (2002) *The Arts and the Creation of Mind*, New Haven, CT: Yale University Press.

Fleming, M. (2012) *The Arts in Education: An Introduction to Aesthetics, Theory and Pedagogy*, London: Routledge.

Freedman, K. (2003) 'Recent shifts in US art education', in Addison, N. and Burgess, L. (eds) *Issues in Art and Design Teaching*, London: Routledge Falmer.

Freedman, K. (2008) 'Leading creativity: responding to policy in art education', in Eça, T. and Mason, R. (eds) *International Dialogues about Visual Culture, Education and Art*, Bristol: Intellect Books.

Gandini, L. and Kaminsky, J. (2005) 'The construction of the educational project: an interview with Carlina Rinaldi (2000)', in Rinaldi, C. *In Dialogue with Reggio Emilia Listening, Researching and Learning*, London: Routledge.

Herne, S. (2009) 'Breadth and balance? The impact of the national literacy and numeracy strategies on art in the primary school', in Herne, S., Cox, S. and Watts, R. (eds) *Readings in Primary Art Education*, Bristol: Intellect Books.

Hetland, L., Winner, E., Veenema, S. and Sheridan, K.M. (2007) *Studio Thinking: the real benefits of visual arts education*, New York: Teachers College Press.

Hickman, R. (2003) 'The role of art and design in citizenship education', in Addison, N. and Burgess, L. (eds) *Issues in Art and Design Teaching*, London: Routledge.

Hickman, R. (2010) *Why We Make Art and Why it is Taught*, Bristol: Intellect Books.

Kindler, A. and Darras, B. (1997) 'Map of artistic development', in Kindler, A. (ed.) *Child Development in Art*, Virginia: National Art Education Association.

Moran, M.J. (1998) 'The project approach framework for teacher education: a case for collaborative learning and reflective practice', in Edwards, C., Gandini, L. and Forman, G. (eds) *The Hundred Languages of Children*, London: Ablex Publishing Corporation.

O'Farrell, L. (2010) *Second World Conference on Arts Education. Final Report.* United Nations Educational, Scientific and Cultural Organization. Online. Available at: http://www.unesco.org/new/fileadmin/MULTIMEDIA/HQ/CLT/CLT/pdf/ Seoul_Final_Report_EN.pdf (accessed 1 May 2012).

Ofsted (2009) *Drawing Together: Art, craft and design in schools.* Online. Available at: http:// www.ofsted.gov.uk/resources/drawing-together-art-craft-and-design-schools (accessed 10 May 2012).

President's Committee on the Arts and the Humanities (2011) *Reinvesting in Arts Education: Winning America's future through creative schools.* Washington, DC. Online. Available at: http://www.whitehouse.gov/blog/2011/05/12/reinvesting-arts-education-winning-america-s-future-through-creative-schools (accessed 10 May 2012).

UNESCO (2006) *Road Map for Arts Education. The World Conference on Arts Education: Building creative capacities for the 21st century.* Online. Available at: http://www. unesco.org/new/fileadmin/MULTIMEDIA/HQ/CLT/CLT/pdf/Arts_Edu_ RoadMap_en.pdf (accessed 1 May 2012).

2

The Way Forward for Science Education

Ivor Hickey

Introduction

In recent times science education has been subject to more intensive scrutiny and revision than any other aspect of education, with the possible exceptions of literacy and numeracy. Very many reports from governments, inspectorates and academic bodies, as well as a large number of academic papers, have addressed all areas of science education practice from nursery school to the efficacy of teacher education. These studies can be grouped under two distinct headings, the provision of science teaching in schools and the broader question of what science education should consist of. There are obvious interactions between the two, but whilst the former can be viewed in relatively objective terms, the latter is more philosophical in nature, although in the long run, clearly more important.

In England, a recent Ofsted report (Ofsted 2011) concludes that there has been an improving trend in the provision of science education, particularly in secondary schools, during the period 2007–2010. This report is typical of many that have been recently produced by inspectorates or equivalent bodies throughout the western world, which indicate that considerable efforts have been made in many countries to address what has been seen as an important but uniquely difficult area of education. There is no doubt that the reported improvements can be seen in a strongly positive light, but it is clear from many international studies that this improvement in classroom delivery of science is only part of a much wider complex of issues about education in the sciences. Over the last 15 years research effort has centred on a number of questions:

- Why educate young people about science?

- What aspects of science should be taught?

■ Which pedagogical approaches are most appropriate to deliver science education?

The aim of this chapter is to explore what the goals of science education could be and how these might be achieved within the constraints of school programmes and the capacities of typical teachers. It will focus on weaknesses in current classroom practice and how improvement in pedagogy is central to making science a more relevant and exciting subject for learners.

Background

The current organisation of science education in the UK is the result of a series of initiatives and these will be outlined briefly. It should be remembered that science is a relatively new area of education and has had a history of having to compete for its place against the traditional subjects. There has been a longstanding attitude, which has only recently receded, that the term 'educated' relates to a broad knowledge of the arts and humanities. Science, itself, may be partly responsible for this attitude. As Stephen Jay Gould suggests, science has tended to regard itself as 'a new kid on the block' and be somewhat aggressive in its relations with the humanities (Gould 2003: 16). This is, in part, a result of the evolution versus creationism debate, which still continues today. However, this division between science and other forms of education has serious consequences for society because science is often seen as an activity undertaken only by selected groups of people. This isolation of science is evidenced by the relatively small numbers of politicians or leaders in industry and commerce who possess degrees in science subjects. This has influenced the development of science in education, resulting in science education being rather self-serving with a strong emphasis on the production of future scientists and maintenance of subject specialities.

Although acceptance of science as a curriculum subject goes back to the latter part of the 19th century, it can be argued that science education was not really taken seriously until after the Second World War. During the 1950s and 1960s, the typical school science subjects of physics, chemistry, botany and zoology (the latter two later fused to become biology) became universally taught by secondary schools. However, technology was regarded as distinct and was usually taught separately as a vocational subject. Often this was even in separate institutions such as technical colleges. The situation has only been reversed in the last 20 years with Technology and Design becoming much closer to the educational mainstream as part of the current STEM (science, technology, engineering and mathematics) initiative.

The 1960s saw strong governmental support for science education, particularly through the recognition of technology as a core area of economic activity by the Wilson government of 1964–1970. In this decade science was formally introduced into the primary curriculum through a number of initiatives (Harlen 2008). The Nuffield Foundation was a major influence in this, and also in the support of secondary science. In both these areas, discovery learning was championed. The next two decades saw a continuation of governmental support and initiatives for science education that culminated in the various statutory curricula implemented by each of the regions across the UK during the 1980s. It is interesting to see how these curricula place science within the curriculum in slightly different ways. For instance, primary science and technology are integrated with geography and history under the learning area of The World Around Us in the Northern Ireland Curriculum, while in the Scottish Curriculum for Excellence, the Sciences are a distinct curriculum area.

Why teach science?

In order to teach science in an effective manner it is important that both teachers and curriculum designers have clear understandings of what they are trying to achieve with their learners. The endpoint in education is ultimately defined by the reasons that the subject is included in the curriculum. Recent studies have examined this matter in some detail, evaluating a number of the commonly held views why science is a vital component of children's learning.

Currently, the most widely employed argument to support the importance of science in the curriculum is simply the economic need for scientists to fill jobs in research and development, those that support health care and other activities that underpin the current lifestyle of western civilisation. This case is made in several governmental reports (European Commission 2004). It is perceived by governments that there will be a serious shortfall in numbers of scientists in future decades unless learners opt for the sciences in increasing numbers. If we assume that this argument is correct, it would imply that science is a more vocational element of the curriculum, which would lower its status as an academic subject, separating it further from the other curricular subjects. It is also likely that this rationale would make it increasingly difficult to present science as an appealing subject, because there would be strong pressure to define such teaching by the content required for learners to succeed in employment. This would likely lead to even earlier specialisation in schools. The fact that increasing numbers of learners find science unattractive as a school subject (Sturman et al. 2008) is already a significant problem and will be discussed below.

As well as providing a potential gateway to employment, science education undoubtedly benefits learners through developing their practical ability to take part in an increasingly technological world. Understanding of even the basics of science is of significant help to individuals in a range of general day-to-day activities, including storing food, checking fuses, removing stains and selecting a healthy diet. Although these may appear relatively trivial, the ability to solve problems by working logically through a series of alternatives based on scientific knowledge may be of great importance in increasing personal happiness and improving quality of life across the whole population. Clearly science is already a major factor in many aspects of personal development education. However, the major justification for the inclusion of science as a prominent subject at all levels within the curriculum is that science now occupies the predominant role in the progression of our culture, and without a firm footing in science students will struggle to appreciate the world in which they live and how it may change. In this sense science should be seen as a narrative rather than a series of lessons that concentrate on explaining specific scientific principles. The subject forms an excellent basis for demonstrating the progression of ideas in human history and their positive or negative impacts on society.

This argument for the importance of science in the education of all children, whether or not they intend to take up scientific occupations, is espoused in many studies and reports from the science education community and is usually referred to as scientific literacy. Scientific literacy is a concept that has been developed over the last half century and unsurprisingly is capable of being interpreted in several different ways (Roberts 2007; Osborne 2007). A useful explanation of scientific literacy is given by the Program for International Student Assessment (PISA), which assessed science literacy in 2006. PISA 2006 defines scientific literacy in terms of an individual's:

- Scientific knowledge and use of that knowledge to identify questions, to acquire new knowledge, to explain scientific phenomena, and to draw evidence-based conclusions about science-related issues.

- Understanding of the characteristic features of science as a form of human knowledge and enquiry.

- Awareness of how science and technology shape our material, intellectual and cultural environments. For example, can individuals recognise and explain the role of technologies as they influence a nation's economy, social organisation, and culture?

- Willingness to engage with science-related issues, and with the ideas of science, as a reflective citizen.

(OECD 2007: 21)

The assessment of learners' scientific literacy that PISA carried out involved questioning within a framework that included real-life situations involving science and technology; identification of scientific issues, ability to offer scientific explanations, use of scientific evidence; understanding of scientific concepts and the nature of science, and interest in science (Bybee et al. 2009).

The thought that scientific literacy should be the mainspring of science teaching is exciting because it will allow teachers to introduce science in a more relevant way to learners and hopefully will elicit a positive response since it deals with matters that impinge directly on students' experience of life. This approach has been developed in current science curricula such as Twenty First Century Science and Public Understanding of Science (Hunt and Millar 2000). However, widening the concept of what is relevant in science learning may cause difficulties for teachers and teacher educators.

What aspects of science should be taught?

The actual nature of science makes its definition as a curricular subject a matter of considerable difficulty when compared with disciplines such as languages or history, because it comprises both the knowledge gained from scientific study and the process of study itself. Separation of factual knowledge from process is relatively simple, but intense debate has taken place over the nature of the processes involved in scientific study. For many non-scientists, including primary teachers, science is defined as a body of facts determined empirically by observations and tested by experimentation. This is often simplistically referred to as the scientific method, consisting of a scientist inducing a hypothesis to explain observations and then testing this through experimentation. However, current academic attitudes stemming from the work of Popper and Khun in the middle of the 20th century see science in much more relative terms, recognising that it has a much more tentative nature. Schwartz and Lederman (2008) state that scientific knowledge is subject to change; its empirical evidence is influenced by current scientific perspectives and personal subjectivity. In addition, they claim that scientific knowledge requires the input of creativity and imagination and that the direction of scientific research is influenced by the society and culture in which the research is carried out. A dramatic example of the last point would be the development of genetics in the early Soviet Union and the bitter dispute between Vavilov and Lysenko that was so closely aligned with the political culture of the time (Roll-Hansen 2005). In addition, it is clearly naïve to assume that all scientists, working across the diverse areas of science can adhere to the same method of research.

This dichotomy of views about the basis of the subject has significant consequences in both primary and secondary science education. If students are encouraged to believe the science that they are learning is an unassailable body of facts, they are likely to become disillusioned and confused when they encounter new theories that cast doubt on the knowledge they have already embraced. In addition, this approach often influences teaching styles, drawing the teacher into a situation where they feel that learners are dependent on them to supply the 'correct and only answer' in every situation. By contrast, if children learn science in an environment that demands creative responses from them as they construct their knowledge of scientific processes and facts, they will identify with science as the current best explanation for the world they live in and be able to adapt to progress in science. Unfortunately, few undergraduate science courses include specific modules on the philosophy of science and this subject is very unlikely to be encountered in a primary teacher's undergraduate programme of study. Even though all current curricula make a clear separation between factual content and development of scientific skills, it is difficult for teachers to maintain the balance of process and factual knowledge. The latter tends to win out because it is easier to assess and allows for a more formal approach to classroom organisation. Significantly, the Association for Science Education (ASE) in their submission to the Cambridge Primary Review point out that a constructivist pedagogy should be employed in science education (Alexander 2010: 225). This stresses the importance of children's creativity in learning science.

In primary education many teachers lack an in-depth familiarity with the workings of science. This results in a tendency to rely on oral and visual teaching of science with, at best, teacher-led demonstrations or practical activities with little depth. Often these involve investigations that are clothed as scientific but that are so simple that most children already know the answer. In secondary education, time, cost and assessment often forces teachers to play down the methodological aspects of science, concentrating on the factual. There have been distinct attempts to move curricula forward to fully embrace the nature of science. One important example of this is the inclusion of 'How Science Works' into science curricula (Toplis 2011). How Science Works corresponds with the PISA definitions of scientific literacy and plays a part in widening the school science curriculum to make it more relevant to learners. However, developments such as these pose problems for teachers and it will require progress in relevant pedagogies and assessment procedures before significant advances can be made. Key to these is the introduction of relevant teaching strategies within teacher education institutions.

Negative classroom experiences in current science teaching

There is a considerable weight of evidence from surveys such as TIMSS (Trends in International Mathematics and Science Study) showing children's interest in science drops alarmingly between the ages of 10 and 13 (Sturman et al. 2008). This subsequently affects the choices they make when selecting subjects to specialise in during their later years of schooling. Additionally, it is well documented in the ROSE project (Sjoberg and Schreiner 2005) that interest in science education is lowest in developed countries. These findings suggest that our science classrooms are not found to be stimulating places by typical children. This is hardly surprising. An equipment-packed school science laboratory may be exciting at first glance, but the joy will soon wane as learners get used to the fact that they are generally performing tasks 'experiments' for which the answers are already known by the teacher. Science rapidly becomes a matter of getting the correct result, or explaining the experimental results you should have obtained from experiments that were designed solely by the teacher. This is not to ignore the vital aspect of practical work, where students learn to handle and operate equipment effectively and gain a sense of confidence in carrying out laboratory work. It is widely reported that children's preferred method of learning science is through practical and fieldwork classes, and has led to calls for more practical work in science.

Theory classes are less popular than practical work. This dislike has been reported to be a result of excessive transfer of factual material from teacher to pupil. There are obvious areas of science where this must be the mode of learning, particularly in relation to safety or description of complex structures or relationships, e.g. the Krebs Cycle or the structure of the solar system. However, science is a hierarchical subject where new information is built on existing knowledge and a much greater effort should be made to allow learners to be involved in gaining knowledge in conjunction with their teachers. Edward Jenkins (2007) makes strong reference to the importance of involving the pupil voice in science education. Other problems encountered in science learning include the fact that as the level increases the dependency on mathematical procedures also increases. This is obviously the case in the physical sciences, but biology can no longer be described as a descriptive subject and certain areas require significant mathematical competence. At one time this would not have presented a problem, but competence in number can no longer be taken for granted. This means that many students have to depend on rote learning of proofs and protocols, even where the teaching is of high quality.

In the primary classroom, science, where it is not part of a national assessment, is generally enjoyed by children (Murphy and Beggs 2003). However, where is it taught in a wider context – for example, in environmental study – there is a tendency for the science content to be obscured. This is often because a teacher lacks confidence in science or finds other environmental and social science topics easier and more satisfying to teach. Much good work has been done in supporting teachers through CPD (Continuous Professional Development), but sometimes this has the unfortunate effect of providing teachers with some effective lessons, but not providing enough background for them to discuss broader topics such as the nature of science. To a certain extent this is a constant dilemma for primary teachers who are expected to have roughly equal competences in all curricular areas. However, the current focus on literacy and numeracy should offer fertile ground for the development of classroom science to provide enjoyable subject material for children to avail of in developing literacy and numeracy skills. This topic will be revisited later.

Transferring school, particularly between primary and secondary, can cause problems in many areas of education and there is extensive evidence that this is also the case for science. Similar problems can arise at other educational interphases and even between school and university. Several factors are important here. Secondary schools often do not have high enough expectations of their new arrivals and tend to repeat work that has already been covered in primary school. A number of useful initiatives have been employed to attempt to bridge this difficult transition, often involving cross-phase teaching by teachers from both sectors (Stephenson 1999).

Improving the delivery of science in the classroom

This is clearly a time of crisis in science education and the solutions are going to be found through changes to classroom practices. Classroom practice follows on from the structure of curricula. Hopefully, the significant changes to context-based teaching of science, as typified by the Twenty First Century Science and Public Understanding of Science curricula, will create a new dynamic within classrooms. It has been shown that Twenty First Century Science significantly increases the proportion of pupils taking science options post-GCSE, indicating a greater enjoyment of the subject by learners (University of York 2009).

A context base for teaching also facilitates integration of the separate science subjects because it is difficult to approach any specific situation from the standpoint of only one of the sciences. At present, even in primary science courses, it is easy to see the separation of physics, chemistry and biology into distinct areas. It is rare to have teachers of different science subjects interact even in connection with integrated topics such as photosynthesis, where complex physics and chemistry concepts are vital for full understanding of the biology.

The primary curriculum would benefit greatly if it was realised that the function of primary science and technology is to interest and inspire children in science rather than teach them basic facts. Several current UK curricula mention the value of children being impressed with the natural world and developing a sense of wonder, but this does not form a strong theme. Current science pedagogies do not allow children sufficient opportunities to express their wonder, or any other emotions, in relation to the world they are studying or to any satisfaction they obtain in the study.

A move to greater discussion in science classes would be welcomed. This is particularly relevant to primary and early secondary education. Importantly, discussion allows room for children to bring their own experiences to the fore, provides a basis for argumentation, allows teachers to set research tasks to answer questions raised by the class and to deal with commonly held misconceptions of science. The latter is recognised as a significant problem, particularly, but not exclusively, in primary classes. Concept Cartoons (Naylor and Keogh 2000) can be used as a way to initiate discussion in class and can often lead to design of investigations. Provided the professional skills of the teacher are utilised in regulating and focusing discussion, science objectives can be met at the same time as supporting children's entire learning experience.

Children's enjoyment of practical lessons and fieldwork has been mentioned before. It is important to utilise these areas appropriately. They can be used to develop pupils' technical skills, including microscopy, setting up equipment, species identification or simple measurement. These science-specific skills must be seen to be valued and assessed, otherwise children will see no point in developing the relevant expertise. Practical activities also have an invaluable role in affording children first-hand experience, which is essential if meaningful learning is to take place. This leads on to the carrying out of investigations where students play a significant part in design. Simple procedures such as deciding on appropriate controls for experimental work and fair testing in the primary class are invaluable for developing students' awareness of the nature of science.

Fieldwork is a particularly endangered but vital part of pupils' experience of science. At present there is serious concern at all levels about the diminution of work outside the classroom (House of Commons Children, Schools and Families Committee 2010). Outdoor learning is not limited to biological or environmental sciences, but visits to factories, farms, power stations, sewerage disposal works, science centres and planetariums represent important opportunities for learning that may be more meaningful for children. However, these visits need to be genuine learning experiences skilfully linked into schemes of work. The Children, Schools and Families Committee noted that 'Learning outside the classroom is strongest at the end of Key Stage 2 ... timetabling trips at the end of the year limits the educational and learning opportunities that can stem from them', suggesting that the maximum impact was not obtained from these events. This is often the case, as trips are often put at the end of a programme of study rather than early on as a stimulus to inform learning. A closely related topic is the use of experts within the classroom. At all levels of education, this is an important but underused aspect of learning. Giving children the opportunity to meet actual scientists is vital for the development of science learning and the production of future scientists. It dispels the common myths about scientists and humanises the subject in a way that little else can. Teachers often expect that experts are unlikely to be interested in being involved with schools, but the truth is very different. Most if not all, environmental, health and conservation charities have education officers who are very keen to get their message across to children. The same is true of many manufacturers, government agencies and university departments, as well as learned societies. In addition, many of these bodies have funds for schools (primary and secondary) to undertake relevant investigations.

At the end of most classroom activities in science lies the task of recording findings. For many teachers this means resorting to the traditional format of introduction, materials and methods, results and discussion. Children find this the least enjoyable aspect of science work (Murphy and Beggs 2003). This method of recording dates back to the late 19th century and although it has its uses in formal and professional science, it is much too cumbersome for most modern applications in school science. Reporting in class requires a more sensitive approach that allows learners to link their scientific discoveries with creative means of communication. Poster presentations make a viable alternative to the formal report and reflect what actually happens at most science conferences. Asking older students to show their knowledge through constructing their own concept cartoons is an excellent way to assess how they cope with misconceptions of scientific principles.

Teachers can be constrained in their approaches to teaching by national patterns of assessment for science because these will set the standard for all summative assessment. It has been claimed that 'Current assessment methods narrow students' learning experiences, in sharp contrast to the broad view of learning goals endorsed in many government documents' (TLRP 2006: 10). Assessment is always a difficult subject, but it must be hoped that testing of practical skills will become an important part of summative assessment. It would be difficult to conceive of music or art examinations that did not included rigorous testing of practical abilities and the same is true in languages. A greater emphasis on practical examinations, even though this may have cost implications, would ensure that practical learning would be re-established in school laboratories. Theory examinations must cover factual knowledge, but inclusion of case studies and data analysis questions would broaden the focus and allow students to show the depth of their understanding as well as their grasp of factual information. Such a model is provided in Twenty-First Century Science assessments and also models the situation in many undergraduate degree programmes.

A novel model for science education has recently been proposed (Osborne 2011). In this the author criticises the conventional approaches to enquiry-led school science. He argues that this usually depends on the traditional understanding of 'scientific method' consisting of observation, hypothesis, experiment and conclusion, a structure that is no longer generally accepted as valid by either philosophers or practising scientists. This clearly is at odds with the wide range of scientific practice and methodology that currently exists in scientific occupations. At present, enquiry-based lessons are generally highly practical in the sense of using a 'hands-on' approach. As noted above, this has often been championed as a mode of learning that children enjoy and stimulates an interest in science as a curricular subject. However, this concept has been challenged recently, suggesting that practical classes are seen as fun, but that this does not translate into increased interest in the subject (Abrahams and Sharpe 2010). Osborne contends that science teaching should be much more holistic than this and operate through three main strands:

- investigation;
- developing explanations and solutions;
- evaluating.

He regards these as three distinct but inter-related social practices. It should be stressed that real science is and always has been a social activity, but it frequently appears, when seen through the lens of the classroom, to be a very individualistic, lonely pursuit. Investigation represents the real world where students carry out observation and testing of the ideas that they generate. The findings of these activities are processed intellectually through inductive and deductive reasoning, creativity and problem-solving to develop explanations and solutions. These two processes are continuously interlinked by the very social process of critiquing and argumentation of both data and solutions in an attempt to make progress in the study.

A key aspect of this approach is imagination; the ability to see the world not as it seems to be, but as it could be. This is well known to scientists, but not associated with science by the general public, or even educationalists. Imagination leads to new ways of thinking that can be tested and the conclusions evaluated; a schoolroom equivalent of the peer review system used by academic journals. The whole process leads to significant development in children's literacy as they strive to refine and redefine the meanings of what they have discovered, and is a genuine parallel of typical scientific practice. The knowledge and experience gained in this form of learning can subsequently be used by the learner to appreciate major science-based policy decisions in the future, the very goal of those who wish to increase scientific literacy in the general public.

The questions of factual knowledge and role of the teacher should be raised in relation to this pedagogical approach. Clearly there is never enough time to allow learners to discover all they need to know through investigation. A careful balance must be struck between knowledge that is supplied to, and knowledge that is gained by the learner. Learners today have access to a much greater supply of knowledge than ever before, thus reducing the status of the teacher as a supplier of facts. However, the teacher has a vital role to play in deciding which facts need to be supplied and how the usefulness of the investigative process can be maximised for the benefit of learners. It would seem obvious that this approach to enquiry-led science learning would predominate in young learners but be reduced in later years where there will be technical difficulties in providing sufficiently sophisticated laboratory settings for learners to undertake appropriate investigations. However, the concept of science as a set of social practices must not be lost and ways must be found to evaluate it appropriately in formal assessment of learners.

The model can be extrapolated somewhat by allowing learners to fuse their science learning with that of other subjects. This allows children multiple entry points to science and a multiplicity of ways of expressing findings and communicating with their peers. It also makes science part of their mainstream experience rather than a subject that will only appeal to a minority of learners. Integrating science learning with learning in art is described in other chapters of this book. This fosters much of the necessary 'discovery' dialogue and sharing of thoughts that must take place between children in a positive learning environment. It is remarkable to note how processes are transferable between the two disciplines and this greatly assists the development of key skills by learners.

At first glance this may seem a pedagogical approach that is beyond typical teachers, but this is not the case. In primary and sometimes in lower secondary schools, many teachers struggle with teaching science because the subject matter is outside their area of expertise. The Leonardo Effect approach described here depends less on specific scientific knowledge and more on the ability to support children to use their creative abilities to solve problems. It provides a viable system for teachers to genuinely learn with the class rather than being solely responsible for transmission of accurate information. As such, it plays to teachers' professional strengths of managing learning in the classroom.

References

Abrahams, A. and Sharpe, E. (2010) 'Untangling what teachers mean by the motivational value of practical work', *School Science Review* 92, 111–115.

Alexander, R. (ed.) (2010) *Children, their World, their Education: Final report and recommendations of the Cambridge Primary Review*, London: Routledge.

Bybee, R., McCrae, B. and Laurie, R. (2009) 'PISA 2006: An assessment of scientific literacy', *Journal of Research in Science Teaching* 46, 865–883.

European Commission (2004) 'Europe needs more scientists, Report by the High Level Group on Increasing Human Resources for Science and Technology in Europe', Office for Official Publications of the European Communities. Online.

Available at: http://ec.europa.eu/research/conferences/2004/sciprof/pdf/final_en.pdf (accessed 20 April 2012).

Gould, S.J. (2003) *The Hedgehog, the Fox, and the Magister's Pox*, New York: Harmony Books.

Harlen, W. (2008) 'Science as a key component of the primary curriculum: a rationale with policy implications'. Perspectives on Education 1 (Primary Science) 4–18, Wellcome Trust. Online. Available at: http://www.wellcome.ac.uk/perspectives (accessed 10 January 2012).

House of Commons Children, Schools and Families Committee (2010) *Transforming Education Outside the Classroom*, London: The Stationery Office.

Hunt, A. and Millar, J. (eds) (2000) *AS Science for Public Understanding*, Oxford: Heinemann.

Jenkins, E. (2007) 'School science: a questionable construct?', *Journal of Curriculum Studies* 39, 265–282.

Murphy, C. and Beggs, J. (2003) 'Children's perceptions of school science', *School Science Review* 84, 109–116.

Naylor, S. and Keogh, B. (2000) *Concept Cartoons in Science Education*, Sandbach: Millgate House.

OECD (2007) *PISA 2006: Science Competencies for Tomorrow's World, Vol. 1*. Online. Available at: http://www.oecd.org/document/2/0,3343,en_32252351_32236191_39718850_1_1_1_1,00.html (accessed 24 April 2012).

Ofsted (2011) *Successful Science: An evaluation of science education in England 2007–2010*. Online. Available at: http://www.ofsted.gov.uk/resources/successful-science (accessed 27 April 2012).

Osborne, J. (2007) 'Science education for the 21st century', *Eurasia Journal of Mathematics, Science & Technology Education* 3, 173–184.

Osborne, J. (2011) 'Science teaching methods: a rationale for practice', *School Science Review* 93, 93–104.

Roberts, D.A. (2007) 'Scientific literacy/science literacy', in Abell, S.K. and Lederman, N.G. (eds) *Handbook of Research on Science Education*, 729–780. New York: Routledge.

Roll-Hansen, N. (2005) 'The Lysenko effect: undermining the autonomy of science', *Endeavour* 29, 143–147.

Schwartz, R. and Lederman, N. (2008) 'What scientists say: scientists' views of the nature of science and relations to science context', *International Journal of Science Education* 30, 727–771.

Sjoberg, S. and Schreiner, C. (2005) 'How do learners in different cultures relate to science and technology? Results and perspectives from the project ROSE', *Asia Pacific Forum on Science Learning and Teaching* 6, 1–16.

Stephenson, P. (1999) *Improving experience in science during cross-phase transfer*, Leicester: SCIcentre.

Sturman, L., Ruddock, G., Burge, B., Styles, B., Lin, Y. and Vappula, H. (2008) *England's Achievement in TIMSS 2007 National Report for England*, Slough: NFER.

Toplis, R. (ed.) (2011) *How Science Works: Exploring effective pedagogy and practice*, London: Routledge.

TRLP (2006) *Science Education in Schools*. Online. Available at: http://www.tlrp.org/pub/documents/TLRP_Science_Commentary_FINAL.pdf (accessed 6 May 2012).

University of York (2009) 'Success in encouraging teenagers to study science'. Online. Available at: http://www.york.ac.uk/news-and-events/news/2009/encouraging-science (accessed 23 April 2012).

3

The Leonardo Effect: Rationale, Methodology and Mechanism

Deirdre Robson

Introduction

The Leonardo Effect isn't for anyone content with the status quo in education, who sees no reason to change the learning landscape. It is for teachers who believe low achievers have untapped potential and high achievers shouldn't be contained. It is for individuals who believe education should excite children and equip them to meet challenges with ideas and confidence. It is only for those who are prepared to think differently, because the journey begins with art.

Quite frequently I observe that children's making of art is not informed by knowledge or experience. It should, because *informed art-making* is good art practice. Leonardo da Vinci demonstrated the full potential of exploiting this when he questioned and explored without the impediment of subject barriers, in preparation for creating some of the world's most venerated masterpieces. Considered a genius, he particularly extolled the virtues of first-hand experience, recognising it was fundamental to his investigations of the world, essential to inspiring questions and fuelling the development of his ideas (Nicholl 2004).

He brought together art, science, engineering and design in a range of creative pursuits, developing skills and producing outcomes that would not have been possible while working within the margins of individual disciplines. Leonardo da Vinci was an interdisciplinarian, and there is justification for emulating him in children's 21st-century education. Drake states: 'With Interdisciplinary learning, the emphasis is on understanding what we learn, which is demonstrated by what we can do with what we learn. True understanding is shown by the transferability of skills so that students can solve new problems in diverse settings. Understanding is increased by connecting to the real world' (1998: 17–18).

There is a compelling argument that learning within disciplines alone is unsound, because it fails to optimise learning opportunities, making it unlikely to best equip young people for their future life and work. On a wider scale, 21st-century challenges have little respect for discipline boundaries, as Newell explains: 'The economic and technical forces that continue to drive globalisation create conditions of increasing complexity and scale that require an interdisciplinary approach to understanding and coping with twenty–first century life and the myriad of problems it presents' (2010: 370).

Art education

I have always found children enthusiastic about expressing themselves in art. To be able to transport this enthusiasm to literacy would please most teachers. I also see children 'bursting' with questions when presented with first-hand experiences in art, eager to know what, how and why; perceptive at making observations and capable of concocting the most ingenious ideas and explanations. Opportunities for dissolving disciplinary boundaries, for educational benefit, abound. Art lessons, which are genuinely informed by first-hand experience and knowledge, and provide time for children to take their ideas forward, are profound learning experiences. They naturally incorporate aspects of the wider curriculum, especially science and literacy. They draw on pupils' and teachers' abilities to synthesise information and develop their creativity, but I believe such opportunities go largely unrecognised.

There may be many reasons for this. Art is not a priority in teacher education in the UK and continues to be squeezed out with financial cuts by government. In primary education, discrete literacy and numeracy lessons dominate the curriculum, limiting scope for education in the true sense. The allocated hour per week for art, often scheduled for a Friday afternoon, indicates 'lowest priority status' and as such it tends to be seized upon for fun–related craft activities at the end of a long week of 'real work'. In post-primary, it is not the art teacher's role to explore other disciplines such as science, particularly in the limited time allocated, so disciplines working together in this context is challenging. However, attitudes to art education are probably the greatest obstacle. What art contributes to human capacity, well-being, industry, culture, the economy, as well as its role in developing children's affective and creative domains is sadly undervalued in our education system.

Connected learning

Aside from craft activities often associated with celebrating festivals, art activity in primary schools generally relates to what pupils are learning about elsewhere in the curriculum, especially now that connected learning is recommended practice in UK curricula. However, the arts suffer badly under the umbrella of connected learning and any increase in depth of learning is questionable. Snyder expresses the view well in saying that 'a connection is the most popular, most used and least meaningful way of linking disciplines' (2001: 35). It is demonstrated where children make copies of Viking runes during art and sing songs about Vikings during music, to reinforce learning in history. Snyder pinpoints the problem using music as the example: 'children are supposedly learning through music, but not learning in or about music' (2001: 34). This similarly applies to art, and it is alarming that such shallow learning experiences are considered acceptable. It may be because concepts and skills related to the arts were not part of the teachers' own education. Snyder says: 'Classroom teachers are comfortable using connections because they require no music understanding and very little skill' (2001: 34). If this is true, the situation is being exacerbated by the progressive removal of art and music from teacher education degrees. It is not surprising that those who practise the arts often despair about connected learning. Connected learning can further marginalise the arts by increasing misunderstanding of them, while failing spectacularly to cater for the needs of pupils in respect of their artistic aptitudes.

Yet children's learning experiences can be deepened and have more value, with relevant input from other disciplines. Children have much to gain from learning in an interdisciplinary manner. Boix-Mansilla comments 'Interdisciplinary learners integrate information, data, techniques, tools, perspectives, concepts and/or theories from two or more disciplines to craft products, explain phenomena, or solve problems, in ways that would have been unlikely through a single disciplinary means' (2010: 289). Unfortunately the potential for exploiting children's natural curiosity, stimulating dynamic ideas and adding to their knowledge and understanding is largely squandered.

Origins of The Leonardo Effect

The idea for The Leonardo Effect interdisciplinary methodology arose out of art and science as disciplines demonstrating potential for mutually beneficial interaction.

I am sure many art teachers find themselves regularly asking students to draw upon their knowledge of science during art, particularly in the study of nature. In discussion with a science colleague, commonalities began to arise: the importance of observation; the emphasis on experimentation; the creativity applied to fields of study that were similar in both disciplines, and the fact that art classrooms were not unlike research labs, both showing signs of inquiry and unfinished study. We discussed the possibility of delivering the two subjects synchronised in some way, with neither playing a supporting role. It was through this that we developed a model named 'synchronised integration' (Robson et al. 2005). Initially we were unaware that 'synchronised integration' could be classified as a form of interdisciplinary teaching, until much later when we learned of Drake's (1998) criteria for interdisciplinarity: exploration of ideas, skills and processes common to different disciplines. Placing the commonalities of art and science at the heart of our interdisciplinary model, we subsequently gave it the name used in schools today: The Leonardo Effect.

Interdisciplinary education

In the 1930s John Dewey was vocal in objecting to a fragmented curriculum being detached from real life, but the origins of interdisciplinary teaching can be traced back even further to the 1920s, when it first began to appear in American universities. It is now common in American universities, including Stanford and Harvard, where it has been established for decades. The Association for Integrative Studies has been publishing on interdisciplinary research for over 30 years. From the 1990s onwards, interdisciplinary teaching became more prevalent in American schools, coinciding with Drake's writing on interdisciplinary teaching (1998, 2007). Reggio Emilia sets the standard for interdisciplinary practice in early years education, and Education Scotland (2012) is now recommending a balance of interdisciplinary teaching in schools across a term, year and phase. It is the first region in the British Isles to specifically do so.

It is something of a conundrum to find interdisciplinarity firmly established within higher education from the humanities to medicine, but not so in children's education. This may be partly due to the autonomy universities have in terms of course design, compared with the greater rigidity of curricula in schools and in particular post-primary schools, where learning and teaching is driven by examination of discrete disciplines, ironically for entrance into higher education. Sir Ken Robinson frequently speaks of the outdated design of our school education system. Millions listen and admire his wisdom, but little action is taken by policy makers. Another powerful figure, the chairman of Google, Dr Eric Schmidt, is reported as saying: 'education in Britain is holding back the country's chances of success in the digital media economy . . . . He said the UK needed to bring art and science back together, as it had in the "glory days of the Victorian era"' (Douglas 2011: np). Within the primary sector, interdisciplinary teaching is slowly emerging, most notably in Scotland and Wales assisted by new curricula. Within post-primary education, change will be difficult until the hold over teaching, learning and timetabling by examination assessment is reformed. However, the potential for progress is now in place.

An exploration of the interdisciplinary research related to education (including the following works: Fogarty 1991; Drake 1993, 1998, 2007; Drake and Burns 2004; Klein 2005; Martinello and Cook 2000; Merickel 2003; Jacobs 1989; Kysilka 1998; Stokroki 2005) reveals no single recommended mode of delivery and few exemplars. The danger is that with a gradual move towards interdisciplinary teaching in the UK, educators will gravitate towards cross-curricular teaching, with its inherent superficiality. The interdisciplinary theory, however, agrees common features:

- Boundaries between disciplines dissolve.
- Constructivist approach.
- Experiential learning.
- Theme or question at the centre.

- Student choice.

- Embedded transferable skills.

- Disciplines connected by common concepts and skills.

- Teacher's role as facilitator.

- Increased creativity from teachers and learners.

- Methods used which engage all children.

- Culminating activity that integrates disciplines taught.

- Accountability and assessment.

(Adapted predominantly from Drake and Burns 2004)

We diversify from the aforementioned list with the addition of art being fundamental to our interdisciplinary approach. It accommodates children's need for self-expression, broadening accessibility for learners by recognising visual learners, who can feel side-lined in a traditional classroom environment. We place emphasis on creativity and informed art-making to enable pupils' creative aptitude to succeed, creating outcomes of value for art and science, which would not have been possible, had the disciplines remained separate. When designing The Leonardo Effect, we surmised that the multiple access points inherent in art experience would entice children to learn about science in an equally unintimidating way, making science more accessible and therefore reaching pupils of all ability levels. This proved to be the case.

Most gratifying for teachers, parents and pupils is the increased engagement with literacy and improvement in literacy attainment. In some cases the results are quite astonishing, showing that through synchronised integration of art and science, literacy levels improve naturally. Pupils respond with curiosity and purpose to the factual and imaginative contexts to which they are exposed, which draw out literacy skills with ease, and commitment to literacy improves without exception in boys and girls.

Education Scotland communicates explicitly to teachers in Scotland the advantages for pupils engaging in interdisciplinary learning:

- learners are more motivated and involved;

- they demonstrate an inquisitive attitude;

- they develop confidence in facing challenges, both intellectual and practical;

- learning is related to real-life experiences;

- it allows more in-depth exploration of topics, issues and problems with and across disciplines;

- it promotes critical thinking and it supports the skills for learning, life and work.

(Adapted from the Education Scotland website)

Foundation for interdisciplinary art and science

In support of a symbiosis between art and science, the late physicist David Bohm believed that it was adults who created the unnatural separation between art and science, which children did not. He said, 'they [children] are gradually trained to think, feel, and perceive in terms of this kind of separation' (Bohm 1998: 80).

Bohm, through his extensive correspondence with the artist Charles Biederman, explored commonalities between art and science. He took as his starting point man's 'fundamental need to assimilate all his experience, both of the external environment and of his internal psychological process' (Bohm 1998: 27). This is certainly true: artists and scientists grapple with attempts to understand and interpret all manner of things, through pulling together knowledge, experience and creating new ideas. They use metaphors, apply logic and intuition interchangeably, visualise, take risks and so forth. This is represented in their manipulation of new information, manifesting itself in an assortment of forms. They share an inherent 'curiosity' to know, to understand and express. They are in effect both researchers and innovators, as was Leonardo da Vinci.

Dynamic collaborations between artists and scientists are rapidly increasing globally. Some recent collaborations are listed below:

- In April 2012, Massachusetts Institute of Technology (MIT) was awarded $1.5M by the Andrew W Mellon Foundation to support the proposed Center for Art, Science and Technology. The grant will provide funding to develop cross–disciplinary courses, research and exhibitions that span the arts, science and technology. It will advance their leadership in integrating the arts into the curriculum and research of institutions of higher learning.

- In 2010 CERN launched a Cultural Policy for Engaging with the ARTS: Great Arts for Great Science. One of its main strategies Collide@CERN was launched in August 2011, with scientists and artists paired so that each could learn from the other's world view, benefiting CERN's research as much as its cultural programme.

- SymbioticA Biological Arts in the University of Western Australia was established in 2000 and is world-renowned for on-going collaborative art science research such as Victimless Leather, part of the Tissue Culture and Art Project.

- In the UK, artist/designer professor Helen Storey and chemist professor Tony Ryan are collaborating in creating Catalytic Clothing, clothing that acts as a catalyst to break down pollutants in the air.

- The Science Gallery in Dublin is a centre that initiates exploration of ideas and collaborations between artists, scientists, educators, engineers and others. In 2011 it received one million euro from Google.org – the software giant's philanthropic arm – to kick-start a network of eight similar centres around the globe.

■ Le Laboratoire and its 'ArtScience Labs' is a network of culture labs founded by Harvard professor David Edwards that catalyse idea translation through art and design experiments at frontiers of science. ArtScience Labs engage, through cultural experimentation, thousands of urban teens and university students each year around the world.

■ Ars Electronica FutureLab in Austria focuses on the future at the nexus of art, technology and society. It considers its works as sketches of possible future scenarios in art-based experimental forms, aiming at developing contributions through methods and strategies of applied art and science, to reveal new knowledge and experiences of societal relevance in art and science.

Wilson says, 'The future will be enriched if this expansion of zones of interest becomes a part of the definition of art and science' (2003: 3). Edwards (2008) describes the crossover between art and science as a remarkable kind of catalyst to innovation that sparks passion, curiosity and freedom to pursue and to realise challenging ideas. Yet, apart from our own work, observations of curricula across the British Isles reveal little evidence of any collaboration or interaction between art and science. This was first brought to attention by C.P. Snow in the Rede lecture of 1959 'The Two Cultures and the Scientific Revolution', where he made a critical comment with implications for educationalists:

> There seems to be no place where the cultures meet. I am not going to waste time saying this is a pity. It is much worse than that. . . . at the heart of thought and creation we are letting some of our best chances go by default. The clashing point of two subjects, two disciplines, two cultures – of two galaxies, as far as that goes – ought to produce creative chances. . . . The chances are there now. But they are there, as it were, in a vacuum, because those in the two cultures can't talk to each other.
>
> (Snow 2003: 16)

Snow identified a problem created by separation and specialisation, which still exists in schools and particularly in post-primary schools. He saw it as a barrier to our creative thinking and achievements. Echoes of Snow can be found in The Association for Science Education's submission to The Cambridge Primary Review on the condition and future of primary education in England. 'Murphy and Beggs report on . . . need for greater relevance of science activities to real life. This is more easily achieved in broader topics than when science is taught as a separate subject' (ASE 2007). Alexander reported in The Cambridge Primary Review, 'as children move through the primary phase, their statutory entitlement to a broad and balanced education is increasingly but needlessly compromised by a "standards" agenda which combines high stakes testing and the national strategies' exclusive focus on literacy and numeracy' (2010: 493).

Commonalities shared by art and science

In proposing to bring the two disciplines together in children's education, we felt a responsibility to identify how compatible art and science were, beyond our own frame of reference. Therefore we sought to identify commonalities. The following commonalities provide the foundation for 'synchronised integration' of art and science. To date we have identified six main categories of commonality:

1. fields of study;

2. modes of inquiry;

3. experimentation;

4. creativity and imagination;

5. visualisation and representation;

6. aesthetic experience and intuition.

Category 1: Fields of study

Biological, anatomical, environmental topics have shown themselves to be common to both art and science. Most curricular science topics lend themselves to exploration and expression in art. For example, pupils investigating, recording and experimenting with: mould and decay of food at first-hand and under the microscope as part of a study of fungi/bacteria; and change of state involving ice, water and steam through colour, temperature and sound. When art and science combine, the potential for creativity on the part of the pupils is extraordinary, but it does require vision on the part of the teacher to visualise where the journey might take the pupils.

Issue-based topics are now increasingly prominent in the arts and the sciences. Those relevant to both art and science would include healthy eating, personal safety and protecting the environment.

Category 2: Modes of inquiry

Sourcing and gathering information, observing and recording, investigating and analysing, can all be classified as methods of inquiry common to both science and art. Underpinned by the fundamental need to assimilate, Kemp says, 'Many artists ask "why?" as insistently as any scientist. For the artist, as for the scientist, every act of looking has the potential to become an act of analysis' (2000: 3). Inquiry is fundamental. Bradburne describes Leonardo da Vinci as 'the intelligent observer par excellence' (2002: 9). The outcome was an unparalleled understanding of the natural world, which informed all his endeavours including his art. From studying the human body walking, he suggested modifications to the skeleton. From dissecting muscles of the face he understood how we smile and could paint the Mona Lisa. Giving children the opportunity to engage in learning using modes of inquiry without concern for discipline boundaries is motivating, memorable and develops higher order thinking skills. It naturally fosters children's creative thinking and independence. In doing so, children will drive their own learning and exceed teachers' expectations. Providing first-hand experiences is the ideal starting point.

Category 3: Experimentation

Experimentation is of primary importance to both disciplines. This appears clear-cut in science, as it obviously provides the necessary data to substantiate or disprove a hypothesis, and was emphasised by Leonardo da Vinci in the 16th century.

Perhaps because the 'processes' in art are not so clearly articulated, experimentation is less apparent in this discipline. Dewey identified it as an essential requirement of both disciplines and writes with great clarity and insight on the fundamental role of experimentation in art. He speaks of the artist's compulsion 'to be an experimenter because he has to express an intensely individualised experience through means and materials that belong to the common and public world' (1980: 144). Each new piece of artwork requires experimentation or artists would simply repeat themselves. Watching even the youngest children involved in art activity, this element is at work in combination with creative thought. Experimentation, problem-solving, intuition and creativity work in tandem, within and across art and science.

Category 4: Creativity and imagination

In the 1970s Bronowski identified imagination as being common to art and science but emphasised a lack of appreciation for its worth in education. He said, 'Science uses images, and experiments with imaginary situations, exactly as art does . . . to suppose that science does not need imagination, is one of the sad fallacies of our laggard education' (1978: 20).

We agree with Eisner, who makes the point that both scientists and artists 'perceive what is, but imagine what might be, and then use their knowledge, their technical skills, and their sensibilities to pursue what they have imagined' (2002: 198). Ede forwards an interesting thought.

> Scientists weave incredible stories, invent extraordinary hypotheses and ask difficult questions about the meaning of life. . . . They create visual images, models and scenarios that are gruesome, baffling and beguiling. They say and do things that are ethically and politically challenging and shocking. Is science the new art?
>
> (Ede 2005: 1)

Arts@Cern states: 'Particle physics and the arts are inextricably linked: both are ways to explore our existence – what it is to be human and our place in the universe. The two fields are natural creative partners for innovation in the 21st century' (2011: np).

Imagination and creativity present many challenges for teachers who have been tied to a rigid curriculum. The European Commission's survey of creativity among teachers in European schools states:

> Teachers' opinions on creativity in education are stronger than their practices. This implies that there is a lot of room for improvement in the way creativity is fostered in schools. . . . Educational policy documents need to raise awareness on the benefits not only of creativity for learning, but also of linking teaching practices and methods with creative outcomes.
>
> (Cachia and Ferrari 2010: 4)

The Leonardo Effect meets this need.

Category 5: Visualisation and representation

We tend to take for granted the metaphors, models, animations and diagrams used by scientists to represent unfamiliar worlds. For example, Francis Wells, surgeon in Papworth Hospital, Cambridge is known for using patients' blood to draw diagrams in the operating theatre to explain the life-saving procedure he uses to repair the mitral valve in the heart, a procedure he developed after studying drawings by Leonardo da Vinci (BBC Online 2005).

Representation in art prior to the 20th century would have been largely naturalistic if we think of the anatomical drawings of Leonardo da Vinci, but Miller identifies further parallels between visualisation and representation in art and science during the late 19th and early 20th centuries. The example he gives relates to the concepts of space and time, which Braque, Picasso and Einstein were all exploring. He describes a 'shift in representation in art from the extremely figurative or naturalistic art as in the Renaissance to the increasingly abstract art of the late nineteenth and early twentieth centuries. These shifts in art coincided with increased abstraction in physical theory accompanied by transformations in intuition' (Miller 2000: 380).

Visualisation and representation is likely to become increasingly relevant in the classroom of the future as we explore additional and alternative means for children to communicate their ideas and understanding rather than simply through written form.

Category 6: Aesthetic experience and intuition

It is generally accepted that facts, logic, reasoning and analysis belong to the domain of science, while expression, aesthetics and intuition belong to the arts. Perpetuating such assumptions only adds to the on-going divide. For example, if science is taught as a body of established facts, pupils are unlikely to take a personal role in moving science forward fuelled by their own passion and at times intuition. Likewise, analytical, reasoned thinking is embedded in any decision-making process; to assume that this may not have a place in art is misguided. Analytical, reasoned thinking has a role in the arts just as aesthetics and intuition have a place in the sciences.

To support this view, Kemp says, 'At every stage in the process of the undertaking and broadcasting of the most committed kinds of science lie deep structures of intuition which often operate according to what can be described as aesthetic criteria' (2000: 2–3).

Like intuition, aesthetic experience is deeply personal. The beauty of a theory, idea or visualisation energises the emotional and cognitive commitment, thus motivating pursuit of further engagement and assimilation. This experience is familiar to those involved in art and science, and applicable at all levels of involvement, from preschool to professional. It relates to joy of engagement as a driving influence.

Art and science, while individually distinctive, also share many commonalities. In recognising this, the potential for meaningful integration becomes a possibility. Synchronised integration based on a foundation of commonalities facilitates the natural symbiosis of both disciplines.

A mechanism for synchronising art and science

It was imperative to us that our model should retain the integrity of both disciplines, therefore neither would play a supporting role.

We sought a mechanism for synchronising the disciplines, which would be workable for teachers. This came in the form of 'joint' learning outcomes/objectives/intentions, depending on the term used in a particular region. Single learning outcomes, in our view, tend to make genuinely integrated planning and teaching extremely difficult and frustrating. The concept of joint learning outcomes emerged naturally from cognisance of the commonalities, accentuating the interrelationship between art and science. An example of a joint learning outcome related to modes of inquiry might be: 'closely and carefully observe the butterfly using a magnifying glass and discuss what you see with your partner'. (Further examples of joint learning outcomes are included in Textbox 4.3.) In such instances, art and science may be so tightly interconnected within individual lessons that separating them would be futile. However, single learning outcomes should continue to be used, where in the teacher's professional judgement it is best to do so. Schools delivering The Leonardo Effect tend to find it appropriate to remove subject titles from daily use, replacing them with the theme or question the children are exploring.

Conclusion

Across the globe, and well beyond the parameters of school curricula, art science collaboration is becoming increasingly recognised as a force for good. As far as we are aware, 'The Leonardo Effect: synchronised integration of art and science' is the only model for integrating the two disciplines in children's education. The

FIGURE 3.1 Children learn from Leonardo da Vinci's notebooks how to observe and record detail in nature. The skeleton was provided by a pupil. It had been found behind the fireplace at home during renovations

model has been extensively researched, trialled, evaluated and embedded in a growing number of schools and, as detailed in part two of the book, schools using it have come through inspections with commendation. This chapter has sought to show The Leonardo Effect's concrete foundation of commonalities that authenticate bringing the two subjects together, and the mechanism that can be applied by teachers to facilitate this.

From the very beginning we believed the central position of art would help personalise children's learning by allowing pupils' individuality to be a motivating influence. Art and science in combination would facilitate the holistic development of the child and provide them with means to express themselves in a diverse range of ways. The following chapter will show how The Leonardo Effect methodology can be put into practice in schools.

References

Alexander, R. (ed.) (2010) *Children, their World, their Education: Final report and recommendations of The Cambridge Primary Review*, Oxford: Routledge.

Arts@CERN (2011) Online. Available at: http://arts.web.cern.ch (accessed 18 November 2011).

Association for Science Education (2007) *The Primary Review – The condition and future of primary education in England, a submission of evidence from the Association for Science Education*, April 2007. London.

BBC Online (2005) 'Da Vinci Clue for Heart Surgeon'. Online. Available at: http://news.bbc.co.uk/1/hi/health/4289204.stm (accessed 5 May 2012).

Bohm, D. (1998) in L. Nichol (ed.) *On Creativity*, London: Routledge.

Boix-Mansilla, V. (2010) 'Learning to synthesise: the development of interdisciplinary understanding', in Klein, J.T., Mitchum, C. and Frodeman, R.K. (eds) *The Oxford Handbook of Interdisciplinarity*, Oxford: Oxford University Press.

Bradburne, J. (2002) 'Looking for clues, clues for looking', *Welcome News Supplement 5: Science and Art*, London: The Wellcome Trust. Online. Available at: http://www.wellcomecollection.org/explore/science-art/articles/looking-for-clues.aspx (accessed 16 April 2012).

Bronowski, J. (1978) *The Visionary Eye: Essays in the art, literature and science*, London: MIT Press.

Cachia, R. and Ferrari, A. (2010) *Creativity in Schools: A Survey of teachers in Europe, JRC Scientific and Technical Reports*, Institute for Prospective Technological Studies JRC-IPTS, European Commission.

Dewey, J. (1980) *Art as Experience* (Reprint), London: Penguin.

Douglas, T. (2011) 'Google's Eric Schmidt criticises education in the UK', BBC News Online. Online. Available at: http://www.bbc.co.uk/news/uk-14683133 (accessed 10 May 2012).

Drake, S.M. (1993) *Planning Integrated Curriculum: The call to adventure*, Alexandria, VA: Association for Supervision and Curriculum Development.

Drake, S.M. (1998) *Creating Integrated Curriculum: Proven ways to increase student learning*, Thousand Oaks, CA: Corwin Press.

Drake, S.M. (2007) *Creating Standards-Based Integrated Curriculum: Aligning curriculum, content, assessment, and instruction*, Thousand Oaks, CA: Corwin Press.

Drake, S.M. and Burns, R.C. (2004) *Meeting Standards Through Integrated Curriculum*, Alexandria, VA: ASCD.

Ede, S. (2005) *Art and Science*, London: I.B. Tauris.

Education Scotland website. Online. Available at: http://www.educationscotland.gov.uk/learningteachingandassessment/learningacrossthecurriculum/interdisciplinarylearning/about/benefits.asp (accessed 10 May 2012).

Edwards, D. (2008) *ArtScience: Creativity in the post-Google generation*, Cambridge, MA: Harvard University Press.

Eisner, E.W. (2002) *The Arts and the Creation of Mind*, London: Yale University Press.

Fogarty, R. (1991) 'Ten ways to integrate curriculum', *Educational Leadership* 49, 61–65.

Jacobs, H. (ed.) (1989) *Interdisciplinary Curriculum: Design and implementation*, Alexandria, VA: Association for Supervision and Curriculum Development.

Kemp, M. (2000) *Visualizations, The Nature Book of Art and Science*. Oxford: Oxford University Press.

Klein, J.T. (2005) 'Integrative learning and interdisciplinary studies', *Peer Review* 7, 8–10.

Kysilka, M.L. (1998) 'Understanding integrated curriculum', *Curriculum Journal* 9, 197–209.

Martinello, L. and Cook, G.E. (2000) *Interdisciplinary Inquiry in Teaching and Learning*, 2nd edn, Columbus, OH: Merrill.

Merickel, M.L. (2003) *Integration of the Disciplines: Ten methodologies for integration*. Online. Available at: http://oregonstate.edu/instruction/ed555/zone3/tenways.htm (accessed 10 May 2012).

Miller, A.I. (2000) *Insights of Genius: Imagery and creativity in science and art*, London: MIT Press.

Newell, W.H. (2010) 'Undergraduate general education', in Frodeman, R., Klein, J.T. and Mitchum, C. (eds) *The Oxford Handbook of Interdisciplinarity*, Oxford: Oxford University Press.

Nicholl, C. (2004) *Leonardo da Vinci: The flights of the mind*, London: Allen Lane.

Robson, D., Hickey, I., Flanagan, M. and Ellison, B. (2005) 'Flights of Imagination: Synchronised integration of art and science in the primary curriculum', Paper presented at BERA Annual Conference, Glamorgan, September.

Snow, C.P. (2003) *The Two Cultures*, Cambridge: Cambridge University Press.

Snyder, S. (2001) 'Connection, correlation and integration', *Music Educators Journal* 87, 32–41.

Stokrocki, M. (ed.) (2005) *Interdisciplinary Art Education: building bridges to connect disciplines and cultures*, Reston, VA: The National Art Education Association.

Wilson, S. (2003) *Information Arts: Intersections of art, science and technology*, London: The MIT Press.

4

The Leonardo Effect: Putting Theory into Practice

Deirdre Robson

This chapter follows on from Chapter 3, which presented the rationale, methodology and mechanism that constitute The Leonardo Effect. It is intended to help teachers put theory into practice by:

- explaining the four stages with examples of classroom experience;
- discussing planning, choosing topics, devising joint learning outcomes, managing learner autonomy, mapping back to the curriculum and selecting resources.

The chapter includes three case studies contributed by Ms Karen Jones, whose class participated in The Leonardo Effect pilot. Finally, extracts from the external evaluation of The Leonardo Effect pilot are included, giving additional perspective on the important aspects of teacher autonomy and flexible planning.

The Leonardo Effect four-stage structure

The Leonardo Effect provides a structure/framework, rather than a prescriptive programme, thus giving teachers and pupils the freedom to make decisions about learning content and the flexibility to apply and adapt it to their own contexts. The commonalities shared by art and science are naturally embedded within the four-stage structure, therefore teachers need not think about them, in their day-to-day practice.

The four stages in essence follow the path taken by many artists and scientists, including Leonardo da Vinci, in the process of their work: gathering information; developing ideas; creating/applying knowledge; and reflecting. The stages are conducive to purposeful and meaningful learning because they challenge pupils to participate and drive their own learning. The stages draw out the learning process, facilitating more depth and incorporation of skills. Perhaps surprisingly, they work well with very young children as well as older pupils.

Stage 1. Research/observation/gathering information (This supports the commonalities shared by art and science that are associated with modes of inquiry.)

This stage enables teachers to lock on to children's interests and open up the process of exploration and discovery around a topic relevant to art and science. Think of children as 'Little Leonardos' exploring a topic or question such as 'How do plants grow?' It should initially involve multi-sensory experiential learning and gathering information about plants in a wide sense, using all options available to them: from reading books to observing at first-hand; from asking experts questions to taking plants apart; generating their own questions and recording information gathered in a variety of ways. For example: using their own sketchbooks to make drawings, simultaneously noting questions and ideas; taking photographs and/or video; or working in small groups to collaboratively record facts they have discovered, in written form. In a specific example on the theme of 'Heart Machine', pupils had the opportunity to observe a cow's heart obtained from a butcher. It generated an avalanche of questions, which the children enthusiastically recorded in groups with large marker pens on giant sheets of paper.

The methods employed in this stage create multiple entry points to learning, therefore facilitating accessibility to children of all abilities and interests. The breadth of exploration instinctively begins to narrow, as children's imaginations are captured by certain aspects they want to explore in more depth, leading naturally on to Stage 2.

Stage 2. Experimentation and development of ideas (The art and science commonalities present in this stage include experimentation, imagination, visualisation and representation in the expression of ideas.)

As children's knowledge increases, their interest becomes more focused. Expression of ideas occurs and confidence increases, in part due to the experience of having a voice in directing their own learning. Therefore potential for following the children's ideas, carrying out experiments, having discussions, playing with materials, decision-making, building of prototypes etc. present themselves, providing opportunities for sustained in-depth learning and lots of meaningful literacy (Bergin 1999). This requires the teacher to recognise opportunities for learning that capture the interest of pupils. For example: in one school pupils were fascinated by snakes during a visit to the zoo, where they could observe them, touch them and ask the zookeeper questions about them. After a series of investigative tasks, they decided to focus more closely on camouflage and pattern. They were introduced to the work of environmental artists Carlotta Brunetti, Nils Udo and Phoebe Washburn, and then began collecting an abundance of natural materials including branches, twigs, leaves, pebbles, stones, seashells, pinecones and chestnuts. They discussed their shape, texture, colour and tone and experimented with their use in making large-scale patterns in the school grounds. They photographed their own work at intervals during the process and at the end, so that they could discuss and compare it with the patterns on the snakes and the artists' work. Another example involved a group of pupils exploring birds' wings. While doing so one of the children mentioned a nearby suspension bridge. The class became curious about the structure of suspension bridges and wondered if they could apply the principles to designing the wings for their flying creature. They worked through lots of design experiments and testing of materials, in pursuit of achieving their goal. This contrasts with traditional subject teaching, which provides little scope for redirecting learning, and sustained exploration and experimentation, or for learning to be deeply informed by more than one discipline. A very significant aspect of this stage of The Leonardo Effect is that it facilitates the learning process to be substantially 'teased out'. It nurtures and encourages development of children's higher order thinking skills, independence, initiative and motivation. Authentic opportunities for incorporating meaningful learning experiences from other curricular areas such as literacy and mathematics occur effortlessly.

Stage 3. Creation/applying knowledge (The art and science commonalities involved in this stage include imagination, creativity, aesthetic experience and intuition.)

In this stage, the pupils apply their knowledge through invention and creation. In the original pilot this involved children inventing and making imaginary flying creatures or machines, having started with the theme of 'Flight', that they could justify, evaluate and present to others. Pupils are always well equipped to accomplish this stage, as a result of the extensive initial research phase, followed by more focused research and experimentation with ideas in the second stage. An example involves children exploring the theme of 'Living under the Sea'. Pupils designed an imaginary submersible for their class to live in for a week, deep down in the Atlantic Ocean. Before this stage they had: investigated how creatures breath underwater through examining fish gills and lungs, recorded what they could see and feel; created dark and oppressive environments; conducted sound experiments and responded to them by looking at artists' expressive paintings and making marks in paint and pastel. They had also investigated machines that have enabled humans to breath under water, assisted by a visit to a science museum. Asking pupils to apply what they have learned takes learning to a higher level again, and pupils respond enthusiastically to the opportunity because they can be creative, imaginative and relatively independent. The Leonardo Effect corroborates Mallery's finding that 'An integrated curriculum is flexible enough to allow students to research topics consistent with their interests and in varying degrees of depth. Concepts become easier to understand when they are related to the solution of a problem' (2000: 9). As a result of this process we find children exceed teachers' expectations. The recommended process of pupils evaluating their creations not only demonstrates their depth of knowledge, but it conveys the extent to which children have developed their skills including literacy skills, thinking skills and interpersonal skills.

Stage 4. Extension

This final stage is optional, to be used at the discretion of the teacher for reinforcing learning and skills development. Activities cannot be specified in advance, however examples have included: narrated fantasy animations based on the earlier work; play writing and performance. Children have also presented what they have learned at parents' evenings or chosen an aspect of what they have discovered as the starting point for a new Leonardo Effect topic. This stage provides potential for embedding, extending and initiating new learning involving knowledge and skills that cross disciplines. This reinforces learning, while potentially involving the community. Importantly it enables pupils to reflect on what they have learned.

The Leonardo Effect and children's responses

Critically the four stages 'draw out' the learning experience to facilitate more depth. Teachers need to be comfortable with the time allocation required to accommodate this. It appears initially that more time will be required. However, schools using the approach find that once The Leonardo Effect is underway it ties in so many other aspects of the curriculum that time is ultimately better utilised and no additional time is required. The stages provide scope for pupils to be active participants with decision-making roles, making learning more interesting and purposeful. It releases motivation in learners because they are inspired and driven by their own curiosity arising from first-hand experience. Just as we believe Leonardo da Vinci was. For pupils, time spent following their interests without regard for discipline boundaries and pursuing answers to their own questions through research may appear lengthy, but it is always beneficial. Teachers should not try to over-engineer or limit this. Pupils will surprise you regarding their commitment, their level of knowledge acquisition and ability to acquire and retain information.

Ideally pupils should have some input in choosing the first-hand experiences themselves. For example, one school in association with their 8–10-year-old pupils identify the themes or questions they wish to investigate a term in advance, and suggest first-hand learning opportunities. This facilitates pupil input at the earliest stage while giving teachers time to source resources.

Some teachers have asked: 'but how is reading books, or speaking to experts art?' The answer is simple: research is part of the artistic process, it facilitates informed art making, which is an essential component of good art practice. Experience, emotion, observation and information will all feed a child's creative and artistic expression. Pupils' creativity is better nurtured where this is common practice, rather than copying the work of artists or working with templates, as is sadly sometimes the case.

Applying the four-stage structure results in pupils' improved self-esteem because they are expected to have ideas, make suggestions etc., and by the nature of this process their individuality and input is respected and celebrated. As a result, disaffected pupils particularly become more committed learners. In providing learning experiences, which naturally dissolve discipline boundaries, development of skills especially literacy skills, thinking skills and interpersonal skills all occur. A good example of this is given by the first case study.

Case Study 1

An amazing thing happened. I had a large class where a third of the children had learning difficulties. These children had been quite challenging and motivating them to actually participate in language activities had been an issue. However, we soon noticed that during this project these children started to blossom. They began participating keenly in all activities because, all of a sudden, they realised that they were learning things that were of interest to them, and that they were actually showing me the methods that they preferred to use to find information on the subject.

These children were constantly reading and scanning books, information sheets, the internet, newspapers for information, and doing it confidently and enthusiastically. It was of great surprise to me that when six of these children were tested at the end of the 12-week term they had risen two whole reading levels, from level 2 to level 4 in reading. Seeing these children blossom and become confident made me realise that this project was going to have a huge impact on them.

(Karen Jones)

Teachers find that The Leonardo Effect provides a single vehicle through which they can deliver the requirements of curricula, in a holistic rather than a mechanistic manner. It also frees teachers to be creative and apply their professional judgement in the teaching of their pupils. Most teachers find this very enjoyable.

Initially, during the training of teachers, we found apprehension among them when presented with the freedom of a structure, without prescribed content. The prospect of devising content that includes following the ideas of pupils sounds risky. The need to be creative was a challenge for those who felt they were not. Certainly to follow a 'prescribed scheme' would have sat more comfortably with some. However, providing examples to illustrate possible content under each of the stages relieved some of the anxiety and once Stage 1 was underway with the children, the momentum was unstoppable.

Choosing a topic/theme to study

When choosing a topic that is relevant to art and science, we recommend making the choice in association with the children while taking account of the curriculum. Large overriding themes that leave the field of exploration wide open can be very effective, such as Woodland, Weather, Water, Movement or Flight, but the teacher needs to be imaginative to envisage how these might be teased out.

Some single word topics can also narrow the field of exploration too much, too soon, so that the full potential of The Leonardo Effect may not be realised. For example: Trees, Thunderstorms, Ice, Dancing or Ladybirds may sound fine, but we recommend that it is better to start with wide exploration and then narrow the field in response to pupils' curiosity. For example, moving from Insects in the first stage to Ladybirds in the second. In this way, scope for pupils to place their learning in context, identify interests and take ownership is optimised.

Developing the idea of context further can bring topics to life for many children, stimulating interest and engaging imagination. For example, The Forest at Night or Life at the Seashore, or making the topic into a question, for example: What is inside me?

Commonly taught history topics in the UK curriculum such as the Egyptians, the Vikings or the Romans have art and science dimensions, but you will find it challenging to place a history theme at the centre and achieve The Leonardo Effect's depth, which is based on commonalities, development of ideas and creativity. Placing history topics at the core is traditionally associated with cross-curricular teaching that emphasises historical facts and involves loosely connected parts of many other subjects to help deliver this. Where history topics must be selected, try to identify an aspect with potential for study using The Leonardo Effect's four stages to run in parallel, such as Mummification of Pharaohs. This could be explored as part of a Leonardo Effect topic on Preservation or Change of State. This strategy need not prevent children from engaging in activities such as drawing hieroglyphics that would often occur within a topic such as the Egyptians, but see these activities for what they are, primarily reinforcing learning in history, as explained in Chapter 3.

Once a topic is selected, it is obviously wise to find out what the children already know about it. At the very beginning, asking them what they would like to know is of 'some' value, but appreciate that they will have many more questions, that convey greater depth of thought, once they have been inspired by first-hand experiences. They will have a 'need to know' that they bring to the situation. This is the optimum time for writing down questions, ideally by the children themselves, individually in their personal sketchbooks or in groups on large planning sheets for all the class to read.

Planning

Although the children will have a significant role in directing their own learning, it is necessary for teachers to look ahead at possible activities. Teachers should begin the planning process by considering 'potential' learning experiences related to the theme selected, thinking as creatively as possible to include multi-sensory experiences, and without consideration of discipline boundaries. In doing so, they should envisage the direction learning might take across the four stages. The first step is to record these learning experiences on a large planning sheet under three headings, taken from the four-stage structure as shown in Figure 4.1. It is important to use large paper such as A2 size for planning, because ideas will multiply rapidly and may extend to several pages. Remember that these are 'potential' learning experiences only, and should be noted down liberally without concern for practicalities, sequencing or connectedness. There will be opportunity for

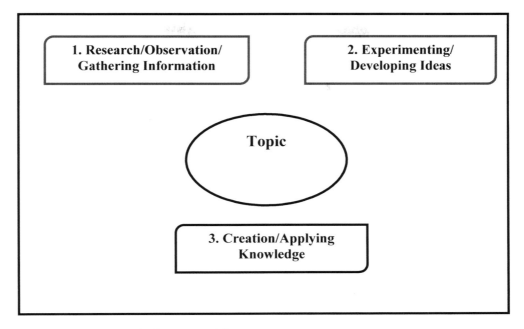

FIGURE 4.1 Planning sheet for The Leonardo Effect

confirming, discarding or developing ideas later, particularly when the pupils begin to show interest in certain directions and express their own ideas, visually, orally and in written forms. It is good to participate in this open–ended process with other teachers, even if individual teachers and their classes choose to explore different topics. Collaborative working is hugely beneficial for stimulating creative thinking and ultimately delivering engaging lessons.

Under the heading on the Planning Sheet (Figure 4.1), '1. Research/Observation/Gathering Information', teachers' suggestions for The Magical Woodland might include ideas listed in Textbox 4.1.

TEXTBOX 4.1 Teachers' suggestions for potential activities that might form part of Stage 1. Research/Observation/Gathering Information, on the theme of The Magical Woodland

Gathering Information

A visit to the wood

■ With eyes closed, listen carefully to the woodland sounds: snapping branches under foot; movement of creatures; birds singing etc. Record the sounds using a sound recorder.

- Touch tree bark, plants, soil etc. Describe what they feel like and write down observations and questions that arise.
- Notice which plants grow in well–lit and shady areas and photograph them.
- Depending on the season, notice tree buds, flowers, seedlings, tree nuts or fallen leaves; note presence of ferns, fungi and conifer cones.
- Record how many birds or other creatures can be seen; look for nests and burrows.
- Look for evidence of animals in partly eaten cones or nuts.
- Look at decomposing logs; count tree rings on felled trees; measure the girths and heights of trees.
- Make sketches of small plants.
- Measure this season's growth on twigs.
- Look at and under logs and leaves on the ground for insects, seeds, leaves, lichen.
- Notice and record all the different sizes, shapes and colours of leaves.
- Observe light penetrating through the trees, discuss, record conclusions.
- Look at the pattern of the trees against the sky and photograph.
- With closed eyes, imagine what it might be like to spend a night in the woods – think of all the words to describe how you might feel and record them in your sketch book.
- Collect small samples from the woodland floor *(to examine under a microscope/ hand lens later)*.
- Collect larger samples such as fallen branches *(perhaps use in environmental sculptures later)*.
- Identify evidence of human activity such as habitation or planting.

Classroom work

- Collate the questions that came out of the visit to the wood and put them on a large chart.
- Investigate Leonardo da Vinci's ideas on trees, branches and growth.
- Read some fiction and non-fiction books set in woods.
- Search for interesting facts on the woodland in books, express them verbally or in written form in groups; make a woodland word bank.
- Look at samples from the woodland floor under the microscope and recreate these using mixed media.
- Make ghost leaves by removing chlorophyll and leaving veins intact.

- Invite a forester, environmentalist, conservationist, wood turner or tree surgeon to talk to the pupils.

- Find out about artists who create environmental art in nature and investigate their work.

- Use the internet to find out about lichens and air pollution, tree bark and creatures that live in the wood. Present your findings using a method of your choice.

- Watch pupils' videos from the visit to the wood and discuss.

- Study artists who captured light streaming through trees and foliage such as the French impressionist Pierre-Auguste Renoir, and recreate the qualities in pastel, using pupils' own photographs.

Ideas will arise for the Developing Ideas or Creation stages while focusing on Gathering Information and these should be added to the planning sheet as well. For example, 'harvest fungi or ferns and make spore prints'; or 'present pupils' photographs on an interactive whiteboard as backdrops for them to act out emotions associated with being in the wood alone. Experiment with images and words to create atmospheric, magical, emotional statements.' Recording ideas in this way as they arise is not possible using the format of a chronological scheme. Importantly, teacher creativity is given scope for expression and this builds confidence, which will ultimately help when drawing out the ideas of the pupils and facilitating creative learning experiences for them.

Some or many of these opportunities may be facilitated, but until the children are involved in the topic, nothing is certain. Additional or better opportunities may present themselves, suggested by the children and expertise possibly made available through pupils 'extended families'. However, teachers should ensure that there is a range of visual, aural and kinaesthetic experiences to meet the needs of all the pupils. In addition, think of potential resources such as artefacts, fictional and factual books, websites, related art works, newspaper articles, television and film footage, to make learning interesting, real and meaningful. The potential for children to be involved in planning is beautifully illustrated in the second case study.

Case Study 2

We asked the children for the very first time to plan their work for the term. They took to this with great enthusiasm and asked if I would also participate in this, so that they would be able to compare their ideas and my ideas by the end of the activity. This was a great starting point for all of us as the children certainly outshone me with their ideas for study areas. Following this activity, both my colleague and myself came together to discuss and study the children's plan and ideas and we were amazed to see that all of the children had planned their work on a question format:

'Do lighter aircrafts fly quicker than heavier aeroplanes?'
'Do clouds fly or float?'
'What is the difference between a helicopter and an aeroplane?'
'Do bees ever fly in straight lines?'
'Are butterfly wings always symmetrical?'
'Does the speed of a bird's flapping wing make it fly higher or quicker?'

The children therefore were clearly showing us what they wanted to learn and how they wanted to learn. We were bowled over by this approach and immediately noticed that the children felt more enthusiastic towards the topic as they had ownership of the term plan.

(Karen Jones)

We recognise that schools have their own planning documentation for schemes, therefore we don't specify paperwork for this. However, the Appendix contains a template for a scheme of work that may be adapted for use. The key factors in a Leonardo Effect scheme of work are: being able to record Joint Expected Outcomes; and space for inclusion of activities under each of the three main stages, which can be drawn upon to devise individual lessons. For example, an activity from Stage 1 and an activity from Stage 2 could be selected to form a lesson. Schemes should never be divided up lesson by lesson for children. They do not learn in neat little packages and it runs contrary to facilitating the development of ideas and pupil input. A scheme should present the macro perspective enabling teachers to see the processes, skills and knowledge embedded over a period of time. We only recommend drawing up a scheme once the earlier planning stage on an A2 page is complete and after the children have had input. Even then it must remain flexible.

We find that for teachers to engage with planning in this open-ended way is liberating and enjoyable. In our experience, the process unleashes teachers' imaginations and creativity and the prospect of carrying out the activities becomes interesting and exciting, as it does in a similar way for the pupils. Even the possibility of exploring the same topic in consecutive years takes on new interest as the children respond with different questions and ideas, reflecting their individuality. It is entirely unlike planning in chronological order using a traditional scheme of work, sometimes delivered to parallel classes, which by its very nature inhibits teachers' and pupils' thinking skills. For some, the greatest challenge initially is thinking creatively, but once teachers begin, confidence in doing so rapidly grows. They also swiftly realise that literacy plays a fundamental part, as do many transferable skills, and soon teachers feel comfortable with being able to take The Leonardo Effect forward with no requirement to plan the content of the Creation stage, confident that this stage will evolve naturally in collaboration with the children.

Support from school management is obviously crucial. It is essential that they understand the methodology and what it means for planning and delivery. An external evaluator's view of the planning process from The Leonardo Effect pilot is set out in Textbox 4.2.

TEXTBOX 4.2 'Teachers' Planning and Preparation' extract from the external evaluation of The Leonardo Effect pilot by the Technology Education Research Unit at Goldsmiths University of London (TERU 2007)

Teachers' Planning and Preparation

The apparently free-wheeling, integrated, learner-autonomous activity . . . might appear to suggest that teachers had abdicated their own responsibilities for planning and learning-management. This would however be a serious misjudgement, for the management of such open learning is a far more complex task than managing straightforward teacher-led learning.

The vast majority of teachers we encountered in the project were brought up on strict, content-led, work-planning processes, and the transformation to Leonardo-like approaches represented something of a shock. And it was scary.

I did not like it very much. From our training days we have been told to plan. I am not the sort of person who takes things as they come. I like to know where I am going and how I am going to get there. Therefore it went totally against the grain not to plan in detail. (Teacher)

The vast majority however soon grasped the nettle and got stuck into planning for joint (and often multiple) learning outcomes that enables integrated experiences to 'hit' outcomes in both art and science.

Initially worrying – not being able to see what was coming next. (but then) Exciting – because I did not know what was coming next. (Teacher)
Head teachers were unanimous about the impact and potential of the project. They spoke at length about how well the teachers had grasped the concept of 'synchronisation' and how well this was working in the classroom . . . it was felt to be what 'good teaching' was all about . . . Head teachers were 'very happy' with this approach . . . teachers beginning to look more closely at curriculum specifications to tease out the joint learning outcomes between subject areas and make these the focus of their attention. (Observer)

Whilst one measure of the success of the project lies in the learning outcomes of the children, the other and perhaps more significant effect is on teachers. We have observed teachers taking real leaps with their own practice, and enjoying the consequence.

Joint learning outcomes/intentions

Joint learning outcomes/intentions/objectives (depending on the term used in your region) are the mechanisms used to enable the disciplines of art and science to come together in individual lessons. Some examples are presented in Textbox

4.3. We strongly advocate teachers using their professional judgement and having the flexibility to synchronise learning where appropriate, and where it is not appropriate, to always recognise this. Teacher-directed lessons should be delivered where a teacher feels the children would benefit from a specific concept being taught this way. In the same way it is important to reinforce the point that joint learning intentions should only be applied where appropriate. They should never be forced. While there are commonalities between disciplines, there are differences too. We also know teachers' time is too precious to squander wondering, 'is it art, is it science or is it both?' It is more important to ask whether the learning opportunity is meaningful, of the highest quality to meet the needs of all children and is it engaging? We also believe that strict adherence to subject boundaries reduces the potential of learning experiences generally. We know it is possible to retain the integrity of both art and science through applying The Leonardo Effect and believe that interdisciplinary teaching offers children more than traditional teaching. Our research and subsequent experience in schools is that joint learning outcomes based on identifying commonalities for art and science not only work, but are beneficial to both subjects without either discipline taking second place.

TEXTBOX 4.3 Examples of Joint Learning Outcomes/Intentions/Objectives (JLO – Joint Learning Outcome) for use in individual lessons

Pupils will:

- Select and consider a range of resources, for example: books, prints, photographs, video to collect information that will assist in the expansion of ideas. *JLO (art, science, literacy)*
- Report findings of an investigation into, for example: thunderstorms; nettles; movement of water; bees using visual and verbal communication to their peers. *JLO (art, science, literacy)*
- Effectively record the butterfly's physical and aesthetic surroundings using a range of appropriate media. *JLO (art, science)*
- Raise questions as a result of exposure to appropriate first-hand experience and communicate these in oral and written form. *JLO (art, science, literacy)*
- In pairs, experiment with paper and card to create structures with height and strength. Test, evaluate and modify as appropriate. *JLO (art, science)*
- Explore the drawings of Leonardo da Vinci to gain an understanding of how he developed and recorded his ideas. *JLO (art, science, history)*
- Identify and analyse strengths and weaknesses in their designs. *JLO (art, science, literacy)*

Managing learner autonomy

When children are given scope to present their ideas, an interesting dynamic develops between teacher and pupils. Teachers listen and can strategically channel pupils in their best interests. Pupils feel they have ownership of their learning and to a large extent they do. This is enough to motivate, and inspire them to show their true potential. The external evaluator refers to managing learner autonomy in Textbox 4.4.

TEXTBOX 4.4 'Managing Learner Autonomy' extract from the external evaluation of The Leonardo Effect pilot by the Technology Education Research Unit at Goldsmiths University of London (TERU 2007)

Managing learner autonomy

It is this topic that presents one of the most profound challenges to teachers. Who is in control of the learning experience? For good learning-management reasons teachers need to be able to steer the project, but for almost every other reason (motivation, developing responsibility) learners need to feel that they 'own' it and that they are making decisions that steer it.

Comments from Children
'very different because we got to decide stuff and it is special because it is unusual that we got to decide some stuff.'

'. . .mostly we could do what we wanted to do – sometimes we needed to be told – things went a bit crazy – too interested in birds, so teacher took us back.'

'we got to choose what we wanted to do instead of teacher saying.'

'We were deciding our own ideas and things to do! For example I chose paper planes and then we made them!'

Comments from a Head teacher
'Child orientated and child led. They were the owners asking the big questions, coming up with their own problems and their own solutions and liked it. . . . The children felt they were in charge, they knew where they wanted to go and how to get there and this gave them confidence – they themselves will be able to say why the 'Curriculum for Excellence' capacities have been met – they are certainly reflective and successful learners.'

Mapping back to the curriculum

We agree with Drake and Burns, who say: 'the educators that actually implement integrated approaches are the same educators who are interested in the most effective ways to teach. They are the ones who constantly ask, "How can I engage all of my students in this learning?" They also are the ones who use the most effective planning strategies such as a backward design process' (2004: 16). This is what we call 'Mapping Back'.

With The Leonardo Effect we are sometimes asked 'but how can you be sure pupils aren't missing out on learning something important?' It is a valid question and it is an example of where the process of mapping back comes into play. Plan a little at a time, see where the pupils go with it and then map back to your curriculum to see what has been achieved. We find that pupils exceed expectations, but where there is a need to reinforce a concept or recap on something that is missed, teachers should go back and teach this in the manner they deem most appropriate. However, when teacher-directed lessons dominate class-time and children are dependent on the teacher's knowledge being transferred to them, then ceilings are set that limit children's imagination, capability and performance. They develop fewer skills and tend to lose interest.

Resources

Providing resources for Leonardo Effect teaching is an important factor for teachers, in addition to finding suitable first-hand experiences, often at little or no cost. Most schools have some budget to allocate to trips, and tend to arrange these for the end of year or at the end of projects, to reinforce learning or simply as a treat for the children. We advocate they should be utilised as a stimulus at the beginning, and if schools cannot afford to take children to a venue, it can be less expensive to bring first-hand experiences and expertise to the children. This can be achieved at a simple level through use of the environment immediate to the school, such as observing birds in the school grounds by establishing bird-tables. It is no coincidence that a Welsh school took pupils to visit a coal mine open to the public that was close to the school, as part of their 'Earth' topic. Forming connections with education officers in relevant charitable organisations and other non-government organisations as well as lecturers in university departments is strongly encouraged; and parents are often the greatest untapped resource in terms of breadth of potential expertise. We recommend informing and involving parents in the topic from the outset. A good example of this is given in the final case study.

Case Study 3

One of our aims was to get more parents involved in their children's education and therefore we corresponded with our parents informing them, that for the term, both the classes were ignoring all school schemes of work and that we were doing what the children wanted to do and learning what the children wanted to know. As you can imagine this immediately grabbed our parents' attention and some even panicked at the thought of it. We then followed this with a letter asking parents to monitor the children's attitude towards their school work, to question them about what different things were happening

---

at school and also set the families a task to participate in any kind of project on 'flight' at home with the children. We gave them a three week period to complete this, including half-term.

We were astounded by the response to this home project. When we returned to school the first day after half-term we had cars and vans all lined up outside the school, and parents whom we had never seen or met before walking into school with their children carrying various models, art work, project folders, aeroplanes with rotating propellers and a huge papier mâché hot air balloon that was even bigger than the child himself.

The response that we received was phenomenal, every single child completing a home project. Following that we were actually inundated with parents offering their services or family members to come into school to help with the project. We had one grandfather who came in, he was the chairman of a local model aeroplane society; he brought with him various planes to show the children, and several children actually visited the society on weekends to fly the planes. We had parents bring in various kites to fly on the school field. We had children who brought all different kinds of flying toys and some keen boys had actually built rockets with their fathers that were made to fly using a bicycle pump.

(Karen Jones)

I have frequently observed student teachers, with a little ingenuity, deliver The Leonardo Effect very successfully without funding, and schools are better placed to be resourceful, build up resources over the years and hopefully allocate a little funding, especially if the school hasn't invested in art materials before. For some schools it will be a new experience to invest in materials that enable children to express themselves visually. However, it is an expenditure that provides children with a vehicle as important to their personal and educational development as any other item of school equipment. Once again it is important that school management commits to this aspect of The Leonardo Effect.

Emulating Experts

Children record information generally in lined school jotters. While these have their purpose, they are limiting. Sketchbooks with blank sheets of paper allow children to express themselves in a multitude of ways, for example: use the pages to record facts; stick in relevant things that they find such as feathers or information they acquire from the internet; draw and annotate their ideas and observations. Think of what would be lacking from Leonardo d Vinci's, Charles Darwin's or David Hockney's notebooks if they were only allowed to write neatly on lined paper. We recommend children emulating these exceptional individuals by keeping annotated sketchbooks, even if they are just in the form of blank pages stapled together by the teacher. Children should be free to use them inside and outside of school lessons. This makes them personal to the child and takes account of the fact that ideas can occur at any time and learning extends beyond school hours.

Children take great pride in their sketchbooks and they become something of a talisman for commitment to The Leonardo Effect way of learning.

The art and science coordinators/subject leaders in primary school also have significant roles to play: ensuring concepts are adequately embedded; terminology is correct; materials, tools and processes are appropriate; introducing teachers to relevant artworks and giving them encouragement to develop their teaching of both disciplines.

Conclusion

This chapter has explained, using a number of specific examples, case studies and extracts from the external evaluation of The Leonardo Effect pilot, how the four stages of The Leonardo Effect translate into school practice, going into some detail on points such as choosing topics, planning and using joint learning outcomes. Creativity and flexibility are emphasised as priorities when planning, and the involvement of art and science coordinators/subject leaders to advise and support teachers, especially in clarifying science concepts and recommending art resources. Scope for learner autonomy and pupil voice is naturally embedded in the approach. From our experience, there are two essential characteristics necessary for The Leonardo Effect to be successful in a school, and these are: motivated teachers who grasp the philosophy of the approach and a supportive management that is prepared to give teachers the flexibility they need to deliver it.

References

Bergin, D.A. (1999) *Teaching and Learning Science: A guide to recent research and its application*, Englewood Cliffs, NJ: Prentice-Hall.

Drake, S.M. and Burns, R.C. (2004) *Meeting Standards Through Integrated Curriculum*, Alexandria, VA: ASCD.

Mallery, A.L. (2000) *Creating a Catalyst for Thinking: The integrated curriculum*, London: Allyn and Bacon.

TERU (2007) *The Leonardo Effect: A research report*, The Technology Education Research Unit (TERU) at Goldsmiths University of London. Online. Available at: http://arrts.gtcni.org.uk/gtcni/handle/2428/15217 (accessed 20 April 2012).

5

Analysis of Feedback from Schools Taking Part in The Leonardo Effect Pilot

Ivor Hickey, Deirdre Robson and
Maryann Flanagan

Introduction and background

In this chapter we discuss the feedback obtained from all those involved in carrying out the NESTA-funded pilot of The Leonardo Effect in primary schools. It includes responses from teachers, head teachers, parents and pupils. The pilot was carried out predominantly with pupils aged seven to eleven in 18 primary schools; of these, eight were located in Northern Ireland, giving a large sample of schools following exactly the same curriculum. Of the rest, two were in Scotland, five in England, two in Wales and one in the Republic of Ireland. This range of geographical locations allowed the impact of the approach to be assessed in schools using related but not identical curricula. Schools selected were from a variety of environments ranging from large cities to small towns and rural settings and from affluent to deprived areas. Two special educational needs schools were included.

In advance of the pilot, two teachers and a member of management from each school attended an intensive two-day training programme, during which they worked through all four stages of The Leonardo Effect structure and experienced the open-ended flexible planning that is essential to this approach.

> The training was designed as a simulation of the experience that teachers would subsequently create for their own learners in their schools. It involved a good deal of hands-on practical experience leavened with enough conceptual and management content to help the teachers grasp the subtleties of what was involved.
>
> (TERU 2007: 7)

All schools took 'Flight' as their topic, interpreting this in unique ways depending on the interests and responses of their classes, and the availability of facilities and resources in their localities. The total time that schools gave to the pilot and how they organised it within their timetables was left to the individual schools to decide. In practice the time allocated varied from six to twelve weeks. During the course of the pilot, schools had regular telephone contact with the researchers and were supported by a number of visits from the research team.

Formal evaluation of the pilot required feedback from all participants and came in the form of:

1. detailed questionnaires distributed to teachers and head teachers;

2. focused interviews with groups of pupils in each school; and

3. a short questionnaire issued to parents.

The questionnaires were structured so that respondents were given the opportunity to comment honestly and in detail on their observations rather than scoring on a numerical system. This was to ensure that full consideration was given to both head teachers' and teachers' professional opinions and also parents' views on this innovative approach to education.

During analysis of the responses received via head teachers, teachers and parents' questionnaires, comments were grouped into three classes:

1. 'positive', where the respondent found that the approach made a positive contribution to teaching and learning;

2. 'negative', where the approach did not; and

3. 'issues', where the respondent found the approach would need to be adapted in their particular circumstance.

The data obtained are presented and discussed by group: teachers, head teachers, parents and children.

Specific areas of the questionnaires are dealt with in detail, with particular emphasis placed on certain comments made by those involved in the pilot.

Teachers' responses

Teachers were issued with a questionnaire consisting of 42 questions, and asked to use their professional judgement to assess The Leonardo Effect approach under a number of headings including: Planning; Teaching; Pupil Learning; Transferable Skills; Development of Literacy and Assessment.

Seventy-two per cent (26 teachers) returned completed questionnaires. There was a strong similarity in the comments made from teachers across the regions. The overall results for the entire questionnaire are shown in Table 5.1.

TABLE 5.1 Breakdown of comments made in the responses from 26 teachers

Positive	Negative	Issues
1,172	0	61

It is very clear that teachers were extremely supportive of the effect the approach had in their classrooms. Strikingly, of 1,233 comments made, no negative comments at all were made and relatively few issues were raised.

Planning

Positive	Negative	Issues
76	0	15

Teachers were challenged in their planning to foster curiosity in their pupils with access to highly stimulating and interesting sensory experiences, to facilitate a range of exploratory and experiential learning contexts, and to plan and work alongside their pupils on the development of the topic. In most cases teachers travelled a journey of discovery with the children, which may not have been possible with traditional planning of lessons.

Despite the fact that The Leonardo Effect asked teachers to adopt a much more flexible and fluid approach to their planning than they may have been used to, the responses were overwhelmingly positive. In fact, many seemed to embrace this concept and found that following the direction of the pupils' curiosity was particularly useful. Statements in response to 'How did you find the open-ended approach to planning?' included:

> Refreshing not to pre-plan, and to listen to the pupils' interests and be led by this.
>
> (Teacher)

> As the project proceeded I found that the planning became more self-evident and presented its own direction via the children.
>
> (Teacher)

In fact, many teachers expanded on this and remarked on the breadth of content that was covered when not adhering to pre-planned schemes of work that take little account of pupils' interests.

> Having no fixed target or end result at the beginning of the project due to its open-ended approach allowed a greater diversity of learning and I feel a much more enjoyable time for both pupil and teacher.
>
> (Teacher)

> Now when I think about the whole year, I feel we have actually covered more.
>
> (Teacher)

There were no negative responses to the questions about planning, although the teachers raised some issues for consideration. These centred on the difficulties of adapting to a new approach to planning. Planning is discussed in more detail in Chapter 4. There are many examples of self-generated questions posed by the children that are less likely to have arisen with more formal planning, such as: 'How intelligent are birds? Where do birds live in East London? What weight is an owl?' Teachers were challenged in their planning to accommodate this level of curiosity.

Teaching

Positive	Negative	Issues
133	0	14

The core of The Leonardo Effect is creativity, and the belief that creative learning and development is dependent on creative teaching. The teachers were asked to reflect on the ways in which The Leonardo Effect influenced their teaching approaches and challenged them to teach more creatively. Typical responses to this included:

> I felt that I was challenged to teach more creatively as the children seemed to be investigating with drawing and modelling a lot more as opposed to reading and writing.
>
> (Teacher)

> I really used the ideas that the children had given me to help me teach more creatively.
>
> (Teacher)

> The children had to think for themselves and work independently of the teacher.
>
> (Teacher)

The final question in this section asked, 'If this new approach was fully supported by curriculum bodies for the long-term, would you be willing to apply it to topics other than Flight?' Generally teachers were very positive about this and highlighted many of the benefits of the approach in support of their responses. For example:

> Most definitely this enthuses children and brings the best out of the teaching and learning experience.
>
> (Teacher)

> I certainly would utilise it as I can see first-hand how much the children have learnt, how much they enjoyed the topic.
>
> (Teacher)

> I think many science topics benefit from being taught this way.
>
> (Teacher)

Although there were no negative responses in this section either, the issues raised drew some attention to a perceived inflexibility in education and centred on the need for educators to learn to change existing and entrenched approaches.

> I feel many of us have been conditioned into focusing too much on what the children know and not how they know it.
>
> (Teacher)

> Each school would have to work together to produce long-term plans to ensure that topics taught like this cover all of the science curriculum.
>
> (Teacher)

Learning

Positive	Negative	Issues
342	0	10

It could be argued that the true test of The Leonardo Effect should focus on the actual learning and development of the pupils. Teachers were asked a range of questions concerned with learning and attainment, and their responses convey the clear message that the approach not only enhanced pupils' learning, but also provided a context where children were more engaged and motivated to learn. Typical comments included:

> Their understanding of concepts seemed beyond what you would expect for their age.
>
> (Teacher)

> I found that the project became a central focus to their school life, many of them watching TV programmes they may have not previously watched, using the Internet for research rather than gaming, and using 'raw' materials, i.e. relatives, family friends, to help and guide them.
>
> (Teacher)

> They were retaining a lot more facts and wanted to learn more about why and how certain things happen in relation to flight, e.g. 'How does an aeroplane fly?'
>
> (Teacher)

Of particular interest were comments relating to the performance of children at different ends of the conventional skills distribution. Answers to the question, 'How did children of below average ability benefit from the project?' were very encouraging because it was widely reported that these children benefited greatly from The Leonardo Effect. A typical quote stated:

> One child in particular who has extensive literacy difficulties enjoyed being able to show the depth of her understanding and analysis of information, through detailed artwork.
>
> (Teacher)

On the other hand, when asked, 'What did the most able pupils gain from the teaching approach?' teachers reported that the challenging nature of the approach was well-adapted to these pupils' needs and that they thrived in such an environment. In addition, the diverse nature of the work meant that 'They had to work together rather than dominate' (Teacher).

The issues represented only 3% of answers and were not focused on any particular area.

Transferable skills

Positive	Negative	Issues
185	0	5

Teachers were asked to comment on the opportunities provided for children to develop transferable skills such as thinking skills, communication skills, ICT and interpersonal skills. Again, the response was very positive and teachers acknowledged that the approach provided a context that was conducive to the development of a range of skills, as pupils came across problems and challenges while their investigations developed. Only five issues were identified. Typical remarks include:

> The project develops children's confidence in communicating with others as many had the oral confidence that comes with truly understanding and owning the material you are presenting to others.
>
> (Teacher)

> Through observation and informal assessment of the children it was obvious that the children were developing thinking skills and their ability to solve the problems they were facing.
>
> (Teacher)

One teacher commented on the exemplification of skills in practice:

> I feel one of the biggest ideas to come out of the project for me was the emphasis on skills rather than very specific objectives.
>
> (Teacher)

Literacy

Positive	Negative	Issues
203	0	9

Although it was not an aim of The Leonardo Effect, it soon became clear to the research team during support visits to schools that teachers had noticed an impact on children's literacy. Questions were included in the questionnaire to ascertain what exactly this impact was. Results followed the usual pattern, with only 4% of 212 answers relating to issues. In the teachers' comments, opportunities for higher order literacy skills and children's motivation to communicate verbally and in written form, featured highly.

Teachers' observations include:

> They wanted to answer their own questions so they wanted to read.
>
> (Teacher)

> Sometimes the quality of the discussion was truly amazing.
>
> (Teacher)

> Children's spellings improved because they were continuously using flight vocabulary. Reading improved during the gathering information period due to children's engagement. Speaking and listening also improved due to children's increased confidence in their work.
>
> (Teacher)

> They are also able to use scientific and subject-related vocabulary in the correct context and they understand the meaning.
>
> (Teacher)

It is clear that an important outworking of The Leonardo Effect was a significant uplift in Literacy. This is reflected in several chapters in the book, in particular Chapters 6 and 12.

Assessment

Positive	Negative	Issues
172	0	8

Teachers were asked how The Leonardo Effect was suited to assessment and how evidence of pupils' art and science knowledge could be observed. Of the 180 answers, 96% were positive. Typical comments included:

> We were able to assess art and science jointly. You can see where the children are using their scientific knowledge through a piece of art.
>
> (Teacher)

Drawings were far more detailed and realistic.

(Teacher)

I feel that I could assess pupils' knowledge of art and science by observing the processes and the products from the synchronised art and science lessons.

(Teacher)

This brief digest of the opinions expressed by teachers to The Leonardo Effect shows unambiguously that, in their professional opinions, primary teachers find the approach to be extremely successful with their pupils.

It is clear that teaching was found to be more creative and enjoyable, and this in turn, created an environment in which pupils' skills were enhanced without the loss of conceptual knowledge. Pupils of below average ability were supported in their learning and teachers observed these pupils become more motivated and gain confidence throughout the pilot. However, the nature of the approach did not hamper the development of high achievers, as they continued to excel. In addition to this, there is strong evidence that pupils' literacy attainment flourished within The Leonardo Effect.

Although a few teachers acknowledged that, in some cases, there were difficulties in adapting their approach to lesson planning using this more creative style, in most cases this problem resolved itself as the pilot progressed.

Head teachers' responses

Head teachers of the schools involved were issued with questionnaires similar to those given to teachers and asked to assess the approach from their school management perspective. In addition to the topics of Planning, Use of Joint Learning Outcomes, Teaching, Pupil Learning, Transferable Skills, head teachers were also asked about the legacy of the pilot in their school and whether they would support the national implementation of such an approach.

Fourteen head teachers returned questionnaires. The overall statistics show that, as found in the teachers' responses, the head teachers made no negative comments and only a few issues were raised. Results are shown in Table 5.2.

TABLE 5.2 Overall responses of head teachers to questionnaires

Positive	Negative	Issues
296	0	10

Of the ten issues raised, six related to the matter of planning, with the following statement a typical example:

Teachers found this challenging as they are used to planning in a more structured way.

(Head teacher)

When head teachers were asked to comment on the legacy the pilot had in their schools all replies were strongly positive, with many reporting that steps had already been taken to adopt The Leonardo Effect, to varying degrees, throughout their school.

> We have changed our whole school planning.
>
> (Head teacher)

> We plan to extend the methodology throughout the school.
>
> (Head teacher)

> Other staff have been very interested and this will have a long-term effect across the school.
>
> (Head teacher)

Again they were unanimously supportive of the national adoption of the approach and suggested that the approach would work with many other topics across the curriculum as it:

> Maintains the integrity of disciplines whilst working across the curriculum.
>
> (Head teacher)

> Parents were amazed by the factual learning as well as the creativity. Children were enthused and parents were delighted.
>
> (Head teacher)

They were subsequently asked what problems might arise for schools if the approach was adopted. Their comments on this centred on planning, as noted above, but also referred to the difficulties providing resources, the workload if the approach was delivered in addition to existing teaching plans, and the need for training.

> The project required a more flexible and creative approach to planning. What do you see as the advantages/disadvantages of this?

Typical comments included:

> It gave the opportunity for children to explore an area in depth. As a result of this, children attained levels in Maths and Science that were much higher than expected for Year 4.
>
> (Head teacher)

> Both teachers and children find it easier to make connections in their learning. This led to much more involvement and enjoyment from the children.
>
> (Head teacher)

Pupils were actively involved in planning for their own learning experiences.

(Head teacher)

The project created much excitement, new knowledge and presented science in a creative approach.

(Head teacher)

The children felt total ownership of the project and fully believed that all decisions about what would happen lay in their hands. They responded very positively to this and the results were quite amazing.

(Head teacher)

. . . teachers have more autonomy and can plan to meet the needs and interests of pupils more effectively.

(Head teacher)

They also raised some points for consideration such as:

This needs careful staff development.

(Head teacher)

Younger teachers trained within the constraints of 5–14 with its rigid adherence to time balance etc. may find it hard to adjust to the creative, flexible nature of planning required.

(Head teacher)

Head teachers resoundingly endorsed The Leonardo Effect, and it was clear that the legacy of the approach would continue in those schools long after the conclusion of the pilot. The pattern of their responses closely parallels that of their teachers; however, they give more weight to the positive effects across the whole school. More detail of the impact that the pilot has had on schools is outlined by head teachers in Chapters 9 and 13.

Parents' responses

Parents of children in each class involved in the pilot were asked to complete a questionnaire consisting of seven questions, which focused on their perceptions of the commitment and response of their child to the approach; whether they supported the synchronisation of art and science in their child's education, and the impact it had on their family.

A surprisingly high number of parents (247) responded. In total they made 1,376 comments and their distribution is given in Table 5.3.

TABLE 5.3 Overall responses of parents to questionnaires. Not all parents who responded answered all seven questions

Positive	Negative	Issues
1,361	10	5

As with the data from teachers and head teachers, there was overwhelming support. There were, however, a number of negative responses. These all related to the following question, 'Pupils worked like Leonardo da Vinci – with first-hand experiences, following their interests, working independently, developing ideas and creating. Would you be supportive of this approach being implemented in children's education?'

Positive	Negative	Issues
216	5	10

Some replies to this question, which we have identified as negative, reflect a cautious attitude. The parents seem to value the approach and see a place for it in education, but alongside the more traditional methods and approaches, rather than in place of them. The five negative answers are recorded below:

> Yes in some lessons like art and science and history but not in maths and English.
>
> (Parent)

> Yes – encourages creativity but would not necessarily suit all.
>
> (Parent)

> I would support working independently and learning through creativity if it were a small part of the school day, however, I do feel that structured lessons are essential in the classroom.
>
> (Parent)

> There should be a structure in place to make sure all pupils attain basic skills.
>
> (Parent)

> No.
>
> (Parent)

However, the vast majority of responses to the question were fully positive and are typified by the following:

> Certainly. The children are learning and retaining facts without realising. It makes the whole learning experience fun and interesting.
>
> (Parent)

Yes, X learnt while having fun. I believe he will remember all the things he learned much better than if the same facts had been presented in a different format.

(Parent)

Yes, I think it would be very good indeed. It would keep the children's minds more active having more interesting topics instead of just English and Maths.

(Parent)

I would be supportive of this being implemented in children's education as it gets them thinking of their own ideas and how they can work on their own, leaving them feeling a sense of achievement.

(Parent)

Yes, I think so. Obviously I'm viewing what went on at some distance but it would appear that this approach succeeded in stimulating the children to think about what they were studying, to explore the themes and have fun being educated.

(Parent)

One other important question asked was; 'Did the project impact on you as a family?'

Positive	Negative	Issues
177	0	2

Several parents made meaningful comments that are worth noting such as:

Yes, he came home from school asking to take him to book shops to buy him books on the subject.

(Parent)

X got us all involved in discussing all the issues and themes she had been exploring in school.

(Parent)

We as a family feel that as a result of the wonderful investigative and creative activities prepared by staff, our children have become more independent learners. They happily use the internet to research Leonardo's work. They are extremely keen to discuss their findings. Many people have commented on their recall of facts.

(Parent)

Despite reservations on the part of a few parents regarding the delivery of literacy and numeracy, the vast majority of parents responded positively to the approach, recognising it as having a positive impact on their children's learning. The research team expected a much higher degree of reservation by parents about The Leonardo Effect, and more concern that literacy should be taught traditionally. Therefore we were particularly pleased to note that parents acknowledged the importance of independent learning, enjoyment of learning, and creativity, and recognised the benefits of The Leonardo Effect to their child's education.

Children's responses

Information from children was obtained during focus group interviews, and the number of questions was limited to allow plenty of interaction. The children were very happy to discuss their views of The Leonardo Effect and a great deal of information was gained. A sample of their comments is included to give an impression of the learning experiences the pupils obtained working through The Leonardo Effect.

There was almost unanimous support for the approach from pupils and when they were asked to describe what they liked about the project, they talked about a range of things. Of 235 comments recorded, we have selected the following:

> 'I like the fact that we can find things out for ourselves.'
> 'Really, really fun and interesting; you learn more.'
> 'Everyone's art got better 'cos we don't normally do it. That is important.'
> 'Made science more interesting – big time!'
> 'Loved doing the science.'
> 'More thinking.'
> 'Brilliant, exciting, amazing, class, great.'
> 'It was a whole different world.'
> 'Doing art and science at the same time, great fun.'
> 'Don't normally like school.'
> 'More freedom.'
> 'We learned more and it was more interesting.'
> 'My favourite part was learning about Leonardo da Vinci. He was an artist – really interesting – not boring.'
> 'Made all this creative stuff – did art – loads more art.'
> 'Fun, educational, interesting, can do all different stuff and you learn more.'

They were also asked to suggest other subjects that they would like to learn about in the Leonardo way. This prompted much excitement and discussion, and across the different focus groups 48 different topics were suggested, with animals of all kinds being the most popular.

> 'Spiders 'n all 'cos I want to learn about them.'
> 'Hedgehogs – nocturnal things – I don't know what they really do in the night.'

'I would like it to be about computers, because I haven't learnt what is inside them and how to build them and how to start a document and games.'
'Human Body – get to learn what's inside you.'
'Art and Maths together.'
'Dogs – there's many types of species and dogs are my favourite thing.'
'Zebras, Dinosaurs, Planets. Mammals, War, Underwater, Jungle, Nature – plants, trees.'
'Making remote control cars.'
'How to make sweets.'
'Animals – zoo, farm, pets, fish, go fishing.'
'The future.'

Their interest in the natural world and investigating how things work became very apparent. This exemplifies the philosophy of The Leonardo Effect, which values most highly children's innate curiosity as a catalyst for learning, then feeding it with activities involving gathering information from first-hand experience, in the same way that Leonardo da Vinci worked. From this starting point, motivation, acquisition of knowledge and development of ideas accelerates. As one child put it to an external evaluator, 'We got to choose what we wanted to do instead of teacher saying' (TERU 2007: 15).

We invited the children to tell us about anything that they did not like, or that they were unhappy about in The Leonardo Effect pilot. It was envisaged that given this opportunity literacy would be mentioned. On the contrary, literacy was not mentioned once. In fact the children did not refer to any particular feature of The Leonardo Effect or aspect of the approach in a negative way. Instead, and rather amusingly, the matters that concerned them are epitomised by the following examples:

'Yes, I did not like that we had to finish the project.'
'It was good when we started, now we're not doing it it's not good.'
'Felt sick on the buses.'
'Some people took credit for things they hadn't done.'

Significantly, not a single child indicated that they would prefer to return to their usual style of learning.

Conclusion

The methods we used to ascertain the views of the various participants in the pilot involved probing the professional opinions of school staff, and more general questioning of parents and pupils. The voice of overwhelming support from the four groups indicates that The Leonardo Effect has had positive outcomes for both teaching and learning.

A number of salient points emerged from this study that are very relevant to development of pedagogy and in turn for teacher education.

It is clear from teachers' responses that The Leonardo Effect supported learning in specific curricular subjects and at the same time enhanced transferable skills development. This meets one of the key requirements of current curricula. Skills development is embedded in The Leonardo Effect, but not at the expense of conceptual knowledge. The significant effect on literacy was also highlighted and is described more comprehensively in Chapters 6 and 12 of this book.

This research has shown that the synchronised integration of art and science is beneficial to teachers wishing to enthuse disaffected or weaker learners, and allows standards to be raised without imposing a ceiling on gifted pupils who have the opportunity to take their learning to higher levels.

From the whole school perspective, head teachers recognised that The Leonardo Effect left a legacy in their schools, both through the achievement of their pupils and in the organisation and planning for future teaching and learning. They recognised the need for teachers to have training to help them adapt to more flexible planning and open-ended learning.

It was also very reassuring that the great majority of parents of children involved strongly supported the approach. It is often thought that parents are mainly concerned with the 'three Rs' and do not see the need for holistic development of their children in primary school. One of the reasons for the positive response from this group was the fact that many reported their children were keen to involve them in what they were doing in school.

Enthusiasm by the pupils for this form of learning came across very strongly in their focus group comments.

Clearly, The Leonardo Effect has been well received by those who experienced it in the pilot. This is well summed up by two quotes from the external evaluation.

> It has been very enthusiastically received by teachers, by learners, and by heads/principals . . . We have seen some quite remarkable examples of positive learning experiences, and we have seen nothing that might be thought to constitute 'off-task' behaviour or attitude by learners.
>
> (TERU 2007: 19)

> Whilst one measure of the success of the project lies in the learning outcomes of the children, the other and perhaps more significant effect is on teachers. We have observed teachers taking real leaps with their own practice, and enjoying the consequence.
>
> (TERU 2007: 17)

The Leonardo Effect provides a way in which teaching can be more successful and enjoyable for learners and teachers while making the required contribution to the achievement of goals set for schools by government.

Reference

TERU (2007) *The Leonardo Effect: A research report*, The Technology Education Research Unit (TERU) at Goldsmiths University of London. Online. Available at: http://arrts.gtcni.org.uk/gtcni/handle/2428/15217 (accessed 20 April 2012).

6

Buried Treasure: Uncovering Literacy Jewels in The Leonardo Effect

Geraldine Magennis and Paula Campbell

Introduction

For a significant number of children, their natural curiosity and enthusiasm to learn appears to diminish as they progress through primary school (Rudduck et al. 1996). Indeed, by the time they reach the age of 10 or 11 years, they have already spent their formative years experiencing a relatively formal approach to education. This dip in eagerness may be due in part to government-imposed curricular demands that prioritise certain aspects of learning over others. For example, an on-going focus on Literacy and Numeracy does not always 'excite' children. Yet it must be kept in mind that enjoyment alone does not necessarily equate with learning. However, it would appear from the data that The Leonardo Effect approach can potentially be a happy bedfellow in furthering key educational outcomes as identified in 'new' curricula throughout the British Isles. The former has attempted to shift from a content-based curriculum to one that is skills-orientated across academic and affective dimensions. Consequently, it is now more conducive to thematic teaching and learning.

The Leonardo Effect takes this integrated approach to a deeper level by identifying commonalities between subjects and creating joint learning intentions with a particular focus on the development of skills and capabilities. This approach is referred to as 'synchronised integration'. Such holistic goals were endorsed regularly within the data obtained from the pilot, with repeated references to participants' heightened interest, elevated motivation, sustained stimulation, active involvement in all aspects of the study and thorough enjoyment. The relevant data are described in more detail in Chapter 5. Many parents championed the integrated teaching of such key themes in this open-ended manner as being both age-appropriate and child-centred. Indeed, a number commented on how they became drawn into the work as a consequence of their child's interest and involvement in it.

This chapter will focus on the most prevalent types of Literacy experienced within the pilot. Although it is an over-simplification of the nature of Literacy to separate out the different strands, it is generally accepted that oral competency underpins the later accomplishments of reading and writing. Indeed, the revised Northern Ireland Curriculum (CCEA 2007) reflects the somewhat newly elevated status of oral language in creating five distinct pillars in the Foundation Stage that form the basis of a broad spectrum of uses.

Talking and listening

Having had their curiosity piqued, children became deeply engaged, having discovered real reasons to talk, listen, read and write. In other words, the purposeful nature of their work resonated naturally with them, resulting in greater self-initiated learning. Teachers noted the most striking increase and marked improvements appeared to be in the children's oral language skills. This was borne out by the fact that in the majority of classes, the usual conversations around the previous evening's television viewing and playground tales were replaced by discussions of both a scientific and artistic nature. The understanding they had gained from first-hand experiences provided within The Leonardo Effect was reflected in their confident use and application of new scientific, artistic and literacy language, knowledge and skills. Perhaps the most obvious and immediate signs of language learning came in the form of attention and listening, following instructions and factual recall.

Listening, following instructions and factual recall

The Leonardo Effect pilot required the children to listen and pay attention not only to the new information they would encounter but also to the 'new' procedures around this learning approach. In some cases, such as during a visit to a bird sanctuary, they were obliged to pay serious attention to health and safety rules in relation to feeding the birds and staying safe around the pond. In other situations, namely when visiting a science centre, pupils were expected to follow directions in order to carry out an experiment showing how aeroplanes take off. They had to make rockets by placing fizzy vitamin C tablets in a little water at the bottom of empty, plastic camera film containers. They then observed as the lids duly sprung off with a loud pop each time. The principle behind this was then explained and directly applied to flight. This aspect was further developed by introducing the concepts of 'friction' and 'aerodynamics', which would be applied to the design of their imaginary flying creatures later. With so much activity going on, the children had to adopt specific roles and learn to cooperate in order to get desired results. Because of having so many opportunities to collaborate and take on various responsibilities, it was noticed how the children 'developed essential team work skills when working in groups. They learnt how to listen to others, make decisions, cooperate and compromise within the group situation' (comment from a teacher).

Frequently teachers commented on the volume of facts children retained throughout The Leonardo Effect. In many cases, this was a result of independent research and peer learning as well as what was being taught in the classroom. It was suggested by one teacher that the richness of the information gathered and the reason why it was so strongly retained was because the pupils were allowed to pursue their own interests. Staff members were continually surprised at the enriched and expanding language that evolved from participation in the pilot (Bergin 1999). Having sharpened their listening skills, the pupils were in a better position to absorb and apply new vocabulary.

Vocabulary extension

New vocabulary was observed when a group of hearing and visually-impaired children visited a bird sanctuary as part of their topic on 'Feathers, Beaks and Feet'. During this visit the children responded knowledgeably to the question 'What kind of birds might you find in a wetland bird reserve?' They knew the names of various birds including 'ducks', 'geese' and 'swans'. This was supplemented by the inclusion of other species, namely 'moorhen', 'coot' and 'Hawaiian goose'. When investigating how birds preen and wash themselves, the children were introduced to contextual words such as 'down' [type of feather], 'rough', 'smooth' and 'soft'. Language that crosses disciplines continued to be reinforced during this session, as the guide equated the 'bones' in a bird's wing with the different 'bones' and 'joints' in a human arm. Later on, one of the hearing-impaired children was heard to relate some of the information he had acquired in the workshop to the real birds he was feeding in the school playgrounds. In another school, when visiting an interactive science workshop, the children were asked 'How do we get up in the air when we fly in an aeroplane?' They knowledgably discussed the role of 'wings', 'forces', 'gravity', 'drag', 'weight', 'lift' and 'thrust', among others. Such scientific terminology was used naturally and correctly during subsequent discussions. Much of this extra language came about through the children asking many questions of their own making.

Asking questions

Assessment for Learning (AfL) procedures outlined in the current curriculum at primary level (CCEA 2007) clearly stipulate as one of its tenets that children should be taught how to generate good questions. This happened naturally in The Leonardo Effect pilot because the children's curiosity led them to seek deeper and in some cases more satisfying answers to their burning questions. A child with Special Educational Needs enquired of a wetland centre's education officer if birds have a sense of taste, while another wondered why a firefly glows so brightly; deep and complex queries indeed. Some teachers also commented on how the relative reversal of roles, whereby the pupils became the predominant questioners, impacted on their professional experience of The Leonardo Effect. For example, in order to facilitate the children to find answers to their own questions, the teachers had to be flexible and spontaneous in their support. As one teacher put it, 'I found that I had to be ready for anything and sometimes to be able to answer a question we would have to make something or try something out; therefore I had to be ready to create.' Often such queries led to further investigations and expansive discussions.

Discussion leading to creative and critical exploratory talk

It was observed repeatedly by the teachers that the quality of ensuing discussions were far superior compared with what was normally expected or indeed occurred. In fact, it appeared that often the conversational dynamic was richer than in a usual teacher question/pupil answer scenario. Typical comments from two teachers are given below:

> There was much thinking aloud going on, and bouncing ideas around which were fantastic to listen to! Sometimes the quality of the discussion was truly amazing . . . I found myself joining in with a discussion quite easily and the fact that I was there did not change the structure of the discussion as might have happened in the past.
>
> (Teacher)

> I've never had so many discussions in my class, that's for sure. I found myself listening to the children a lot more and letting them take the lead.
>
> (Teacher)

'Flight', which was the theme of The Leonardo Effect pilot, was as yet an unexplored topic for the children, and so they became heavily engaged in exploratory talk with their peers. Referred to by Mercer (2000: 16) as inter-thinking, this kind of prolonged or profound thinking about ideas or questioning of reasons, evidence or information (Dawes and Sams 2004: 3) was facilitated frequently throughout The Leonardo Effect pilot. A supportive context was created, wherein collaborative thoughts were formulated, vocalised and interrogated critically when challenged by others or by new information before shared understandings were reached. This very valuable process was alluded to by one teacher, who said, 'The project gave me the opportunity to value much more the experience, the transferable skills rather than the finished product. Everything had to be decided on as a collective.'

Such an exchange of ideas was witnessed during a rich conversation around the differences between male and female duck feathers. One child regaled his peers about how the female's dull-coloured feathers were designed to aid camouflage so that she might remain safe when sitting on her eggs. Conversely, he informed the group, the male duck's brightly-coloured feathers change annually as a means of attracting a new mate. This kind of learning experience where children are accommodated 'to think rationally and to consider and evaluate each other's ideas in a cooperative way' (Grugeon et al. 2001: 95) exemplifies the philosophy of creating informed and independent learners on which the current curriculum hinges.

While each stage of The Leonardo Effect promoted the use of exploratory talk, it was particularly evident in the third stage – the 'Creation' stage. Working collaboratively, children had to express their ideas clearly and constructively argue as to why certain features were appropriate for their imaginary flying creature, drawing on their collective knowledge about flight. They were able to do this admirably. Eight-year-olds were giving explanations of the principles of force and aerodynamics with ease and enthusiasm as if they were knowledgeable adults or even engineers. This was not simply regurgitation of what they had read, because in-depth questioning testified to their abilities to further explain their logic. Phrases such as 'why do you think that?', 'why does it need three beaks?', 'can you explain?', 'I think that', and 'I agree with you' were commonplace among the groups of children. As a result of the numerous, diverse talking and listening opportunities arising from The Leonardo Effect, teachers commented on how this enabled them to assess children's knowledge and understanding more accurately than through written assessment, which they felt might have done some children an injustice.

The presence of creative and critical thinking was strongly felt, particularly in the 'Experimenting' and 'Creating' stages. As one teacher explained:

> The process of designing and making their own camouflage kite, flying it and then evaluating it based on experience involves critical and creative thinking skills. The children were given a variety of materials and challenged to make them fly. When working out how to put the toys together and fly them, the children had to use problem-solving and decision-making skills. Working in groups to make the final flying creature also involved all of the above intellectual skills.
>
> (Teacher)

Of course, all of this oracy was complemented beautifully by reading and research.

Reading

Meaning-making and comprehension

The purpose of reading in general is to 'make meaning from print', otherwise it is a pointless exercise (Browning Schulman and daCruz Payne 2000: 25). This extremely complex and dynamic process is facilitated through the integration of many reading strategies that operate through the informed use of context, language structure and letter/sound knowledge (Pinnell and Scharer 2003). A key aspect of comprehending written text is having the ability to visualise the message encoded in the print and then interpreting and applying that to both school work and life. Understanding the text will also be influenced by the readers' real lives; therefore, it is imperative that pupils have lots of concrete experiences and language to draw on.

These necessary prerequisites were cultivated especially during the 'Gathering Information' and 'Developing Ideas' stages of the pilot because of the emphasis placed on first-hand experience. No matter what the age of the pupils, practical sessions are a common feature of The Leonardo Effect. For instance, when experts visited the participating schools with various winged creatures (e.g. birds of prey), the children were able to experiment, explore and investigate some of the facts they had previously read about. Insights gained were then applied to the closely observed features and movements of aircraft. Their working knowledge of the theory they had read was deepened when they took part in making and testing models of their prototypes.

Regardless of the various sources of information available to the children, one teacher noted that 'Many became obsessed with the wonderful flight books when they were usually reluctant readers.' In one school, a teacher commented on the noticeable rise in the children's enjoyment levels of reading even among disinclined readers. In this same school, the host teacher went as far as to attribute her pupils' increased reading ages with their involvement in the pilot. The variety of texts provided to support the pilot were commented upon positively as an 'excellent' and 'lovely mix of fiction and non-fiction which motivated children to read'. As a result, many children were engaging with books beyond their years, internalising the information and experimenting with their new found knowledge. Following a question and answer session, one teacher expressed her delight at how her pupils were able to retain and recall so much specific vocabulary and self-discovered knowledge with ease. She attributed much of this to the fact that the children found the books on flight interesting and purposeful. However, as pupils mature, it is imperative that they are equipped with higher order study and research skills because they are transitioning from the 'learning to read' into the 'reading to learn' phase.

Study skills, research and digital literacy

Deep and meaningful engagement with interesting subject matter served as a catalyst for the promotion of study skills and self-initiated research even beyond the school day, involving various texts, written materials and technology. A number of parents remarked on this welcome change in their children's study habits. One teacher disclosed that some of her pupils 'ended up doing "mini projects" of their own on killer bees and the Siberian flying squirrel!' Another commented that since the children were given 'freedom to dictate their own learning both in pace and content . . . many were doing their own research, unprompted and with a thirst for more knowledge'. However, study and research skills involve the teaching of advanced and discerning use of the ocean of information available to the researcher. It has to do with modelling how to skim and scan texts for key words and phrases, otherwise wholesale plagiarism of random pieces of knowledge may result. Further to this, it also includes how to skilfully put the collected information together for a given audience.

Unsurprisingly, the Internet was found to be a valuable tool for the children in their own research. It was used by the pupils to search databases for information on a variety of topics from aircraft and birds to recycling and pollution. Numerous websites, on-line encyclopaedias, DVDs and CD ROMs were navigated in the name of information gathering, aide memoires and means of evaluating completed works. Practice in this particular study skill was deemed worthwhile because the children in one school improved throughout the duration of the pilot to the point where they used their acquired knowledge to build a 'branching database' on the computer. Another class extensively used the Internet not only for research but also to disseminate collated information, which was then used 'to assist in the development and construction of their models'. The idea of using the pilot to teach and reinforce the relevant and effective use of the Internet was taken up by a teacher who felt that study skills in this area required attention. In another school a second teacher capitalised on this idea by making two Web Quests as a way of ensuring that all pupils were able to use ICT effectively. In the same school, some pupils produced PowerPoint slides as a visual record of their work and these were used extensively to aid subsequent research.

There is a plethora of other examples of how the children used the various aspects of ICT to enhance their learning. For instance, the Digital Blue camera proved to be an important piece of recording equipment in a number of different ways. Some used it to capture the different stages and developments within their work and such records were put on display for many others to appreciate. In other cases it was used to record interviews and 'to create animations of flying objects', displays and 'experiences in the playground with the toys and the kites' produced during the pilot. It was employed frequently as a method of digitally retaining evidence of various visits and fieldtrips. The video camera was used in a similar way, except it had the added benefit of allowing the children to narrate their work. Both pieces of equipment were utilised by at least one school for the purpose of assessment. Video programmes were also used in an interdisciplinary manner to help inform the children about such happenings as the history of the Wright Brothers' adventures. Having gained so much valuable experience in talking, listening and reading, there was lots of scope now for fruitful and meaningful writing opportunities.

Writing

Visual literacy

In recent years, the importance of visual literacy in supporting teaching and learning has been greatly endorsed in research literature (e.g. Bearne and Wolstencroft (2007)). It is based on the premise that meaning can be derived through interpreting images such as diagrams, computer-generated graphics and digital pictures among others. This approach was evident during the introductory phase when during one school's visit to a science centre the demonstrator presented the children with a labelled sketch of an aeroplane, which was then referred to frequently during the development of the talk. Toward the end of the trip, teacher exposition was used again along with a supporting diagram when the children were shown how to make helicopters out of paper and paper clips. The reasoning behind how this worked was again interrogated and for those children who were having difficulty, they were asked to try and problem-solve their predicament using the knowledge they had acquired. Photo-stories and graphics packages were used to complement their word-processed efforts. Due to the experiential approach having informed their scientific and artistic knowledge, this provided the basis for rich written responses. Such newly acquired knowledge seemed to encourage and empower the children to write of their own accord and this took many forms. One particular type of non-fiction genre that occurred naturally during the pilot was explanation writing.

Planning for explanation writing

Written work is symbolic and therefore a somewhat abstract activity that demands a high level of competence to produce. Best practice would dictate that much discussion and 'messiness' precede the finished article. Embryonic ideas and probing discussions are often moulded and then translated onto paper through the use of graphic organisers [diagrams] and eventually writing frames that help shape the final piece according to the genre being explored. In The Leonardo Effect, there were many opportunities for initial ideas to be jotted down and revised as new knowledge was uncovered. This phase was experimental and so neither the teachers nor the pupils became overly concerned about the secretarial aspects of their work such as presentation, spelling and handwriting. Instead, the focus remained on the content and comprehension of what the children were discovering. Figure 6.1 shows a graphic organiser produced by a child to show their understanding of birds' beaks.

Such annotated diagrams provided support for more detailed note-taking, an intermediary step on the way to continuous prose. Two examples of children's jottings taken during research for explanation writing follow:

> To make their nest comfortable birds pluck off some of their down feathers and place them inside the nest.
>
> (Pupil)

> It takes the buzzard three days to lay one egg. It has very good eyesight but no sense of smell. The second bird we looked at was a peregrine falcon. It was a fast bird. It is the fastest living creature on earth. It flies at 200 miles an hour and eats other birds. Its favourite bird is a pigeon.
>
> (Pupil)

Original 'rough work' and notes were then used to produce longer, more detailed pieces of explanation writing, as shown in Figure 6.2.

This kind of format was true for various other types of writing that emanated from the pilot.

FIGURE 6.1 Planning for explanation writing

Discussion and implications

It would appear that The Leonardo Effect approach to teaching has significant implications for curriculum delivery. Firstly, tapping into the innate reality of how children learn is vital, since by the time a new-born baby enters the world, it already has enormous potential for holistic growth and development. The extent

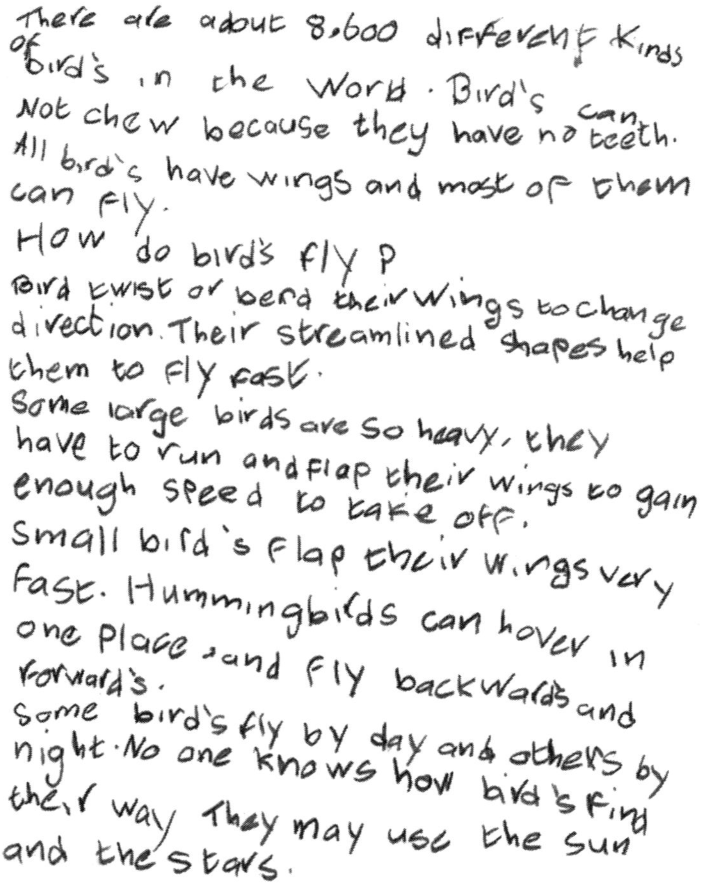

There are about 8,600 different kinds
of birds in the World. Bird's can
Not chew because they have no teeth.
All bird's have wings and most of them
can fly.
How do birds fly?
Bird twist or bend their wings to change
direction. Their streamlined shapes help
them to fly fast.
Some large birds are so heavy, they
have to run and flap their wings to gain
enough speed to take off.
Small bird's flap their wings very
fast. Hummingbirds can hover in
one place, and fly backwards and
forwards.
Some bird's fly by day and others by
night. No one knows how bird's find
their way. They may use the sun
and the stars.

FIGURE 6.2 Example of completed explanation writing

to which this comes to fruition depends on the level of stimulation received and indeed research shows that this process is best aided through multi-sensory stimulation (Bee and Boyd 2007). The pilot had this in abundance in terms of the practical experiences, environments and resources experienced. Indeed, by virtue of its physical design, the brain demands repetition and consolidation of knowledge and skills in a myriad of ways in order to secure embedded learning through ingraining the imprint of neural pathways. When this reality is honoured by interactive, participatory and challenging educational provision, as was the case in the pilot, only those connections that are useful are maintained, strengthened and made permanent (Blakemore and Frith 2005: 18).

However, most of the children in the pilot study from across the British Isles were 7–10 years old, which means that they have received quite a different kind of formal educational experience up until then. This may be viewed with concern

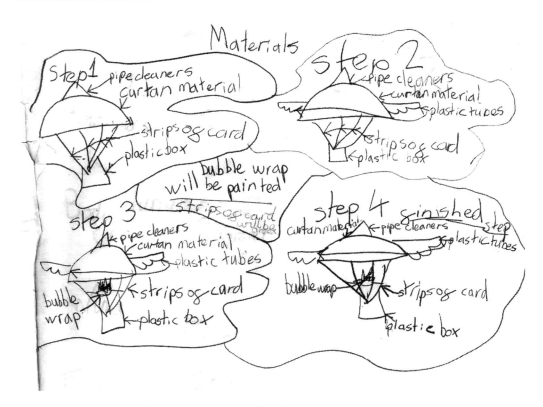

FIGURE 6.3 Example of writing emanating from the 'Creation' stage

by some who believe that the 'windows' (Sousa 2001: 23) in the brain through which information enters and learning occurs do not remain open indefinitely, and so it is imperative to capitalise during 'sensitive periods' (Blakemore and Frith 2005: 26) when learning potential is greatest. Implementing The Leonardo Effect sooner could be judicious since it is thought that early life experiences in particular help shape the brain and design its 'unique neural architecture that will influence how it handles future experiences in school, work and other places' (Sousa 2001: 24). Subsequent to the pilot, this interdisciplinary approach is now in regular use in Early Years classes.

Possibly another reason for the pilot's success is that this approach to study resembles play, which so often becomes neglected as children move up through school. Perhaps much of the positivity vocalised by the teachers, pupils and parents who experienced this form of exploratory education stems from the fact that as humans we are 'hard-wired' to make sense of the world in all of its complexity through the vehicle of play. According to Stuart Brown (2010), the neural pathways that allow learning to occur are restructured and strengthened through play activities, no matter what our chronological age. Not only is this the case but such a state of being is a natural conduit for creativity and imagination, thus increasing motivation.

In The Leonardo Effect, a multi-modal approach engaging all of the children's senses allowed them to experience the various facets of flight. This strengthened their 'knowing' before they were expected to demonstrate such 'knowing' in more abstract ways. For instance, because the teachers did not demand written work as the only or principal measure of what had been learnt, the children initiated writing because they found it purposeful and interesting. Communication in its many and complex forms wove the whole approach together.

By taking part in the pilot, it is clear that divergent learning styles are honoured without having to contrive the context, thus leading to holistic and deeply embedded teaching and learning. Specifically, from the calibre of the conversations overheard throughout the various stages, between and among teachers and pupils, there were repeated opportunities to listen and be heard, to use multi-level language, to read various print forms, utilise an array of media and experience assorted writing genres. Needless to say, uncovering these hidden literacy gems was an extra and extremely welcome bonus for a variety of obvious reasons, none more so than the very recent publication of yet another government document, *Count, Read: Succeed* (Department of Education, Northern Ireland 2011), a strategy to improve outcomes in literacy and numeracy.

Perhaps the on-going taste of success incentivised the children to persevere even when faced with challenges that required further reading and research. So often children, especially those who struggle with Literacy, give up or feel deflated when obliged to continue to engage in literacy-type activities. However, in this situation, it could be argued that, in resembling Craig's 'knowledge community' (Seaman 2008: 271), the pilot provided a kind of wrap-around support for all participants. Indeed, Thomas and Seely Brown (2011: 17) refer to this dynamic as 'a new culture of learning', whereby participants in their research not only learn extensive subject matter via this collaborative approach but they in fact internalise bigger and often more important messages of citizenship and socialisation. Two head teachers particularly mentioned progress made in terms of emotional literacy. One noted that their pupils 'learned to be more tolerant of each other and to appreciate each other's contributions and strengths', while the second disclosed that 'many of the children developed improved interpersonal skills'.

Maybe the less conventional methods of what might be described as 'organised chaos' provided the children with a level of comfort and relaxation about their work that they were able to lay down any performance anxieties in favour of displaying their true abilities. It is only when freedom of expression is experienced in a richly resourced and stimulating context (where time is flexible) that the learner can then function at the neo-cortex level of the brain where multiple cognitive connections are made. Even from the outset, the pupils were deeply involved in that they were instrumental in the planning stages. Although Literacy elements were not specifically planned for, they frequently 'glistened' from beneath mainly scientific and artistic discussions and activities. As the pilot progressed, planning ideas and assessment opportunities continued to evolve naturally according to the evolutionary paths taken by the children's subsequent curiosities and discoveries. One teacher referred to the children's enthusiasm during the planning phase as being 'quite infectious'. As a consequence, teachers began to notice discernible improvements in their pupils' engagement with literacy.

Coupled with this, it could be argued that there was an unconventional swapping of roles between children and teachers. Rather than a rigidly planned set of activities delivered by the teachers in a prescriptive manner, the content and especially the process unfolded in such a way that often the children led the enquiries. This meant that frequently they determined the sources of information to use, the conversations around the concepts under scrutiny and the form of presentation their findings should take. In return, the teachers were able to 'scaffold' the children's efforts and thus bring them up through their individual 'zones of proximal development' (Pound 2006: 40). It could be said that this approach superseded individual policies and planning protocols that so often set down somewhat narrow perimeters within which to teach and learn.

Thomas and Seely Brown (2011: 19) develop the idea of a rich and meaningful environment and approach as being conducive to what they call 'arc-of-life learning' that reflects real life education rather than that which is only contained within classrooms. They argue that this honours the balance between a structured curriculum and the open-endedness of technologically-mediated socialisation. They claim that in order for education to truly serve children in the 21st century, two common denominators must be present and intertwined. The first is unlimited access to a huge information and resource network relating to learning about anything and the other is a structured environment with definitive perimeters. The latter is important because it is only within such bounds that countless possibilities for experimentation with ideas can be fully realised. It is interesting to note that teachers found some of the most knowledgeable children were those who normally wouldn't be engaged or were deemed to have Special Educational Needs. Therefore, might the professionals benefit from interrogating their thoughts on this need for a cultural–educational mind shift rather than the children who embraced the challenges with enthusiasm?

Perhaps the greatest testament to the success of The Leonardo Effect was that Literacy in its many forms was used naturally and seamlessly to serve and be served by the theme of Flight. Just like diamonds or other precious jewels, opportunities for naturally occurring Literacy learning were 'mined' in many ways and showcased without that intentionally being the goal. It was so deeply and intricately embedded in the subject matter that the children probably could only really see the 'fun' and 'interesting' scientific and artistic bits. Strangely, due to the symbiotic nature of Literacy and other subject areas, this 'oversight' was not detrimental to the learning of Literacy concepts and conventions. On the contrary, the avoidance of a discrete 'drills and skills' approach seems to have produced unexpected but welcome dividends.

In conclusion, honouring the awesome design and capacity of the human brain and how young children learn and communicate was surely respected on many levels by The Leonardo Effect methodology. These repercussions seep beyond the academic benefit of subject knowledge and skill-building. They potentially impact on personal development, deepen communication and facilitate transferrable learning not only across disciplines but throughout life. However, the real beauty of The Leonardo Effect is that such Literacy jewels are uncovered like buried treasure rather than forced to emerge. Surely this should be the case in many other parts of more formal curricula in operation across the UK, where practitioners might best serve the standards agenda by identifying those precious Literacy nuggets that lie within authentic and rich learning and teaching contexts.

References

Bearne, E. and Wolstencroft, H. (2007) *Visual Approaches to Teaching Writing: Multi-modal literacy 5–11*, London: Paul Chapman.

Bee, H. and Boyd, D. (2007) *The Developing Child*, 11th edn, Boston, MA: Pearson Education.

Bergin, D.A. (1999) 'Influences on classroom interest', *Educational Psychologist* 34, 87–98.

Blakemore, S.-J. and Frith, U. (2005) *The Learning Brain: Lessons for education*, Malden, MA: Blackwell.

Brown, S. (2010) *Play: How it shapes the brain, opens the imagination & invigorates the soul*, New York: Penguin Group.

Browning Schulman, M. and daCruz Payne, C. (2000) *Guided Reading: Making it work*, New York: Scholastic Professional Books.

CCEA (2007) *Northern Ireland Curriculum, Primary*, Belfast: Council for Curriculum, Examinations & Assessment.

Dawes, L. and Sams, C. (2004) 'Developing the capacity to collaborate', in Littleton, K., Miell, D. and Faulkner, D. (eds) *Learning to Collaborate: Collaborating to learn*, New York: Nova Science.

Department of Education Northern Ireland (DE) (2011) *Count, Read: Success: A strategy to improve outcomes in literacy and numeracy*, Bangor: DE.

Grugeon, E., Hubbard, L., Smith, C. and Dawes, L. (2001) *Teaching Speaking and Listening in the Primary School*, 2nd edn, London: David Fulton.

Mercer, N. (2000) *Words and Minds: How we use language to think together*, London: Routledge.

Pinnell, G.S. and Scharer, P.L. (2003) *Teaching for Comprehension in Reading: Grades K-2*, New York: Scholastic Professional Books.

Pound, L. (2006) *How Children Learn: From Montessori to Vygotsky – educational theories & approaches made easy*, London: MA Education.

Rudduck, J., Day, J. and Wallace, G. (1996) 'The significance for schools improvement of pupils' experiences of within-school transitions', *Curriculum* 17, 144–153.

Seaman, M. (2008) 'Birds of a feather? Communities of practice & knowledge communities', *Curriculum & Teaching Dialogue* 10, 269–279.

Sousa, D.A. (2001) *How the Brain Learns: A classroom teacher's guide*, 2nd edn, Thousand Oaks, CA: Corwin Press.

Thomas, D. and Seely Brown, J. (2011) *A New Culture of Learning: Cultivating the imagination for a world of constant change*, Charleston, SC: CreateSpace.

Case Studies

7

Creativity on Fire in Ynystawe

Carolyn Davies, Lynne Bebb, Gwenith Davies, Sarah Richards and Rachel Parkes

Ynystawe Primary, housed in a stone building over 120 years old, is one of the original Leonardo Effect pilot schools, where the methodology is now firmly embedded. It is a local authority maintained co-educational school serving the established communities of Ynystawe and Ynysforgan villages, situated at the lower end of the Swansea Valley in South Wales. The 200 pupils enrolled come from a wide range of social backgrounds. The school was inspected in 2008, two years after being first involved in the pilot.

Creativity

A creative thread runs through everything staff and pupils do at the school, whether it is in teaching mathematics, English or any other subject. To develop pupils' creative and critical thinking skills and independent learning skills, a whole school approach is taken, where every class adopts a common theme and philosophy, with teachers recognising the importance of continuity and progression across age groups. 'Outside classrooms', within the perimeter of the school grounds, enable a substantial amount of teaching and learning to take place in the outdoor environment, and teachers often take pupils beyond the school environment entirely.

Teachers encourage pupils' creativity, research, investigation and problem-solving skills at all times, and when The Leonardo Effect came to the school it was embraced wholeheartedly, because the philosophy chimed perfectly with that of the school. The school recognised that The Leonardo Effect required teachers to genuinely value and respect children's creativity and also be prepared to develop their own. The methodology presented a way forward where everything that the school believed about working with children could be realised on many levels, both across the school and across subjects, with creativity at the core. The school's

FIGURE 7.1 Teachers and children use the outdoor environment for learning, where appropriate

vision has proven successful because Ynystawe scored grade one in every area of the 2008 inspection, which stated 'Pupils' standards of achievement were judged to be well above the targets set by the Welsh Assembly Government for 2007' (Estyn 2008: 3). Quotes from the Inspection report are included in Textbox 7.1.

Creativity is at the heart of Ynystawe Primary School, but the meaning of creativity can be difficult to articulate in education. Ken Robinson provides a useful interpretation.

> Being creative does usually involve playing with ideas and having fun; enjoyment and imagination. But creativity is also about working in a highly focussed way on ideas and projects, crafting them into their best forms and making critical judgements along the way about which work best and why.

In every discipline, creativity also draws on skill, knowledge and control. It's not only about letting go it's about holding on.

(Robinson 2011: 5)

Creativity in Ynystawe Primary School is probably best described as a bundle of particular attributes. This means creativity is fostered; children typically become risk takers, often producing innovative and alternative solutions. They are self-motivated and have a good concentration span because they are pursuing their own interests. They display curiosity, awe and wonder in what engages them; and are very imaginative. They relish the roles of problem solver and decision maker, and are also able to reflect on their own performances, showing critical awareness. They persevere and show good attention to detail. Their manual skills may not be particularly strong, but they practise in order to develop their skills and bring their ideas to fruition. Creative children are skilful thinkers. Creativity is very much about teachers providing space and time for children to draw together experiences, make connections and think 'outside the box'.

Children thrive in a creative environment, benefiting in many aspects of their development from social skills to acquisition of knowledge, and the application of The Leonardo Effect at Ynystawe exemplifies this. The Leonardo Effect provides the catalyst, while the school, its teachers and pupils are the creative environment in which creativity flourishes.

Towards the end of the pilot, the different threads of experience, knowledge and skills were drawn together and the children were invited to use their imagination to apply all they had learnt to create something new. The result was a flock of flying creatures that incorporated both the natural and mechanical modes of flight. A white creature with owl-like eyes for seeing in the dark had propellers coming out of its head instead of wings. The children were delighted to see their own wonderful inventive creatures suspended from the ceiling in the school's main hall. They were eager to invite their parents to see what they had achieved. Parental support had been positive from the beginning, but the end results were far more than they could have expected.

Following The Leonardo Effect pilot, the children went on to use the methodology to explore the four elements of Earth, Air, Fire and Water as individual themes. For the theme of water, the children spent a lot of time using their senses and observing an array of different types of fish. The children were fascinated by the extraordinary eyes of the fish, the silvery reflective scales and the sinuous shapes. Their observational drawings using colour and line inspired huge collages, mosaics and poetry.

The theme of fire provided opportunities to look at the work of artists such as Welsh painter Mary Lloyd Jones. A detail from one of her paintings that featured a lightning strike inspired individual relief tiles for a large ceramic wall panel. In the school yard a model of old London Town that had been built by the children was set alight as a commemoration of the Great Fire of London. Earlier observation and scientific investigations of actual fire and flames preceded and informed the responses to this conflagration.

Ynystawe Primary School is fertile ground for creativity. The Estyn (Education and Training Inspectorate for Wales) Inspection Report recognised this, stating: 'The innovative curriculum successfully broadens pupils' horizons and provides them with exciting and far-reaching experiences, both within the school and beyond' (Estyn 2008: 3).

TEXTBOX 7.1 Quotations from the Ynystawe Primary School Estyn Inspection Report 2008

Pupils are actively involved in planning their own learning and to pursue their own line of enquiry as is very well illustrated by the 'Leonardo Project'. This is an outstanding example of the holistic approach to the curriculum where key skills are very well integrated and pupils encouraged to become independent learners. (p. 7)

Pupils' numeracy skills, problem solving and creative skills are consistently good with outstanding features throughout the school. This is well illustrated by pupils' work in their 'Leonardo Project' linking the Arts and Sciences in their designs of flying creatures. This demonstrated pupils' exceptionally well developed skills and their ability to use their skills in a variety of contexts. (p. 12)

The provision of holistic learning experiences through projects, such as the 'Leonardo Project', actively encourage the development of children's ability to pursue their own interests and become independent learners and responsible for their own learning. (p. 16)

Art

Unlike many primary schools, art is central and is considered to be of key importance in the appointment of every new teacher. For over a decade the school has appointed people who have art expertise in the belief that if teachers can be creative in art, they will be creative in delivering the full curriculum, with the outcome of motivating learners and bringing out each child's potential. Art is seen as being interlinked with all the other subjects and the ability to see and make connections to achieve this is essential.

Children are given the opportunity to experience many aspects of artistic expression. The question is posed, 'How can children know if they can do something or have an aptitude for a particular skill, material or technique, unless they have had the opportunity to try it?'

Teacher expectations

The staff have high expectations of what young children can do, valuing each child's contribution and the displays and exhibitions throughout the school demonstrate this effectively. By valuing children's contributions, opportunities for achievement are maximised, and in turn, all children are encouraged to reach their full potential. When they are given lots of opportunities to succeed, it is easier to see what they can do rather than what they cannot. Children can work to their strengths, bringing their individuality and potential to the fore and boosting their confidence to tackle areas of difficulty. Before the school was involved with The Leonardo Effect, Welsh Curriculum documents had been put aside and the environment surrounding the school utilised as a theme for learning. Within this parameter children were inspired and as a result able to lead their own learning, with teachers capitalising on what the children found interesting. Teaching concentrated on what the children thought they should be learning about. The results that this strategy produced were convincing, and on analysis it was found that all Welsh Curriculum requirements had been covered through the learning experience. This process of mapping back was also useful when implementing The Leonardo Effect. More, not less, is achievable when creativity is at the core of learning.

The links between this practice and The Leonardo Effect were obvious from the start and the whole school environment provided a stimulating platform that enabled the creative potential of the approach to be realised.

Planning for creativity

The starting point for The Leonardo Effect at Ynystawe is mind mapping, which is a powerful tool for creativity. Through the creation of mind maps children assist with the planning process. The teacher can see what motivates them and is then able to engage the children in discussions that link the areas of intended study with their particular interests. Plans of work are created with the children at the outset of each theme. This significant role in the early part of the process motivates the children and hence the creative bundle of attributes mentioned earlier is allowed to gather momentum. Once this stage has been reached, teachers bring the mind maps to the staffroom to share together.

Freedom to deviate from what has been planned is felt to be very important. For example, during the study of 'Flight', a child whose family were renovating their house discovered the skeletons of some dead birds when they took the fireplace away. The child brought them into school. This created such a lot of interest and led to much work, which originally hadn't been planned. This typifies the flexibility that The Leonardo Effect offers teachers in responding to children's ideas.

It can be challenging to move away from what has been planned. However, it is a different level of planning that is necessary. Often there is pressure from outside agencies, and teachers can be genuinely afraid to change a well-organised scheme of work, but the part of the leadership role of the head teacher is to encourage teachers to strive to focus on the dictum 'stick to how you know children learn'.

Learning environment

Classrooms in Ynystawe are creative. Resources of time, materials and people are managed in a child-centred, flexible and dynamic way. At times there may be no walls, there may be no chairs; there may only be floor space. It can be indoors or outdoors, in a small or expansive space. The classroom becomes a concept that adapts to fit the activities rather than the activities fitting the physical space. In this creative space all children can work experientially. The creative classrooms are stimulating, providing a safe and secure environment in which children can be challenged and motivated. Here a multi-sensory approach to learning is easily facilitated. Individual learning styles are catered for as children can experiment, make choices and work at their own pace. Ynystawe pupils respond well to 'real things'. There were remarkable and unexpected results when the children handled feathers and birds' wings, observing them at first-hand. The work produced was unique and every individual child found expression for their ideas using a wide variety of materials and techniques. This is exemplified in Figure 7.2.

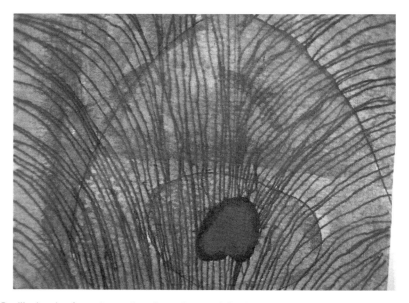

FIGURE 7.2 Pupil's drawing from observation of a real peacock feather

The Leonardo Effect thrives in such a dynamic learning space, but it also requires a flexible, creative curriculum. The creative curriculum at Ynystawe is apparent throughout the school. In every year group, children work as independent learners, deciding at every stage where their interests lie.

A flexible programme of work is another feature of the creative curriculum. For example, the school was involved in the 'Take one Object' initiative at the

National Waterfront Museum in Swansea. The object selected was the Robin Goch (Welsh for 'robin redbreast'), one of the few aeroplanes built before 1914 in Wales that still survives, and one of the earliest examples of aircraft in the United Kingdom. The children visited the Museum to see the aircraft for themselves and discover its intriguing story. This initiative was fitted seamlessly into the original Leonardo Effect theme of Flight.

Visits such as this provide a special experience that gives an enormous impetus to the child's creative learning. Importantly, it is a common experience that acts as a stimulus for collaborative working without reducing each child's own personal experience, interpretation and understanding. During a visit to the Fleet Air Arm Museum in Yeovil, the children responded well to one of the guides, who was very interesting. When he showed a picture of Leonardo da Vinci, all the children made the connection with 'flight' straightaway and were excited that their prior learning had relevance.

The teachers find that such is the excitement generated by this approach that there are not enough weeks in the term. The children set their own priorities and can realise the time constraints for themselves. The creation of whole class mind maps at an early stage helps because they can see that there is so much to do.

Sometimes things can be fitted in, and sometimes not. The curriculum is organised so that The Leonardo Effect is followed from January to July each year and during the autumn there is a basic skills focus. During this term there are stand-alone study weeks, when Welsh Curriculum topics that do not fit obviously into The Leonardo Approach are undertaken. However, whether it is basic skills or The Leonardo Effect, all learning is experiential.

The creative practitioner

In the absence of creative teachers and creative teaching, creative learners will not develop their potential and no amount of curricular or contextual support will have the desired effect. At Ynystawe the staff members learn from each other, so creative teachers can bring creativity out in other teachers. Just like the children, the teachers are continually seeing links and are always making connections. This is a significant aspect of the whole school approach to creativity.

It is important that teachers see the value of what can be achieved through a creative approach such as The Leonardo Effect, otherwise it becomes very difficult to work creatively. To ensure that all staff members are fully committed to the school's approach to the curriculum, high quality, in-house training is on-going at Ynystawe. But it is impossible to have a creative school without a head teacher who believes in its importance, who is supported by an informed governing body.

Assessment

With such a flexible child-centred curriculum in place, in a classroom space that moves, contracts and expands, with deviation from what has been planned, an equally flexible approach to assessment is required. In Ynystawe assessment is on-going, through observation, listening and by outcome. Extensive use is made of photographic records, and comments are recorded throughout the learning process. An observation file is kept for each child and levels of achievement can be determined by reference to the children's sketch books. Portraiture as a theme is seen as a very valuable assessment tool that can be extended throughout each child's school career.

Self-assessment is very important and the staff at Ynystawe use the AfL technique of 'two stars and a wish', which involves children selecting two things that they are happy with and one that they feel they could improve upon. Further records include 'ladders across the curriculum', folders with levelled examples of work from all subjects and records of all the experiences that the children have had each year.

Conclusion

Creativity, characterised as a bundle of attributes, flourishes in Ynystawe, with the application of The Leonardo Effect. The children create wonderful and profound work in abundance, which demonstrates their ability to innovate, take risks and solve problems. The work is both a product and also an indicator of their knowledge, imagination, curiosity and ability to be moved and inspired by what they encounter during the learning process. The quality of the work speaks of their developed critical awareness and aesthetic sensibilities. It is a testament to their thinking skills, their diligence, their concentration and their attention to detail.

But the application alone of The Leonardo Effect methodology could not have created the conditions for such a flourishing of creativity. If the work created by the children at Ynystawe is impressive, then so is the philosophy and vision of the staff that underpins their achievements. It is a philosophy that establishes the rich creative environment that is a prerequisite for any learning methodology that focuses on children's creativity. The aim at the school is to create memories for the children to take with them into the future and it is seen as important that they remember their primary school education in a positive way. The creative space, resources, practitioners and the approach to the curriculum and assessment were in place in the school from the outset and enshrined in the school's visionary statement:

> Our school will endeavour to provide a challenging and stimulating experience-based curriculum for every child, and this in the security of a happy and welcoming aesthetic learning environment.
>
> We envisage all children achieving their full potential as independent learners in order ultimately to take their place in society as confident, tolerant and courteous people.

At all times we strive to promote a culture wherein we feel a sense of belonging and pride in our school and also a belief in ourselves as individual members of both the school and the wider community.

I hear and I forget
I see and I remember
I do and I understand

(Confucius 551–479 BC)

References

Estyn (2008) 'A report on the quality of education in Ynystawe Primary School'. Online. Available at: https://swansea-edunet.gov.uk/en/schools/Ynystawe/Documents/School%20Inspection%20Reports/Inspection%20Report%20Ynystawe%20Primary%20School%202008.pdf (accessed 19 April 2012).

Robinson, K. (2011) *Out of Our Minds: Learning to be creative*, 2nd edn, Oxford: Capstone.

8

Jordanstown School Applies The Leonardo Effect in Teaching with Children who are Deaf or Visually Impaired

Barbara McGuigan and Gail Lawther

The population at Jordanstown School encompasses children from the age of 4 to 19 with sensory impairment, some of whom have additional needs. We were invited to be involved in the national pilot of The Leonardo Effect to see if the approach would work with our Key Stage 2 classes of profoundly deaf and visually impaired children. Two classes took part. One comprised six deaf children; the other was a visually impaired class of eight pupils, two of whom were totally blind and six who were partially sighted with varying levels of useful vision. We were provided with art materials, flight toys, DVDs and some financial help to invite visitors in to the school and to go on fieldtrips. We will describe the work carried out during The Leonardo Effect in two parts. Work with the deaf children is described by Barbara McGuigan and work with the visually impaired class by Gail Lawther.

The Leonardo Effect with deaf children

Initially I had reservations, because I wondered if my pupils could cope with the more pupil-led approach, and if they would be able to communicate effectively together without a lot of guidance. I have been teaching Key Stage 2 pupils for 15 years at this school and our policy is to teach our deaf pupils using an approach called Total Communication. This refers to using all means of communication – sign language, voice, fingerspelling, lip reading, amplification, writing, gesture, visual imagery, to make understanding as clear as possible. The philosophy of Total Communication is that the method should fit the child, instead of the other way around (McDonald Connor et al. 2000).

This involves providing the children with the best listening conditions and technology possible to assist their hearing. We also use 'Signed English' and lip reading to aid communication and understanding. This group of six children aged 10–11 varied in ability, but I knew they would enjoy the new challenge, resources and visits.

The idea of integrating art and science was not a new idea to me. I have been teaching subject areas as topic themes throughout my teaching career. It simply made sense to me to make these connections for my pupils. Examples of topics include: 'The Body', 'Ships and the Sea'; 'Vehicles'; 'Rural versus Urban'. There were four reasons why The Leonardo Effect methodology appealed to me. First, the freedom the pupils would have to follow their own interests and ideas; second, the fact that I would take a back seat and allow them to learn through their own mistakes; third, I would have more time to observe the children and finally, that I wouldn't work from a pre-planned scheme of work, allowing me to be more flexible. I saw my new role as a facilitator, challenger and encourager, quite different from my usual teacher-led set lessons, and I was looking forward to the change.

The Leonardo Effect training gave us some guidance on how to lead the pupils through the pilot. We were introduced to the four-stage model. On 15 September 2006, we started stage 1, 'Observation and Gathering of Information'. This lasted three or four weeks. I began by asking the pupils to share together by physically drawing everything they knew about 'flight'. Drawing helps many deaf children to show, in a concrete way, what they know and also aids oral communication, especially for the less able. One child mentioned having seen a 'flying fish': this gained the children's attention and led to the confirmation that this was true by a search on Google for pictures and information.

Together they created a topic web on flight, which they reviewed at the end of the pilot to show them how much they had learned. I told the children that they were in charge of this project and they had to choose which area they wanted to study first, natural or mechanical flight. Natural flight was chosen and each child was given a sketch book and good colouring pencils to record all the things that interested them. Importantly, pupils got to visit a local animal sanctuary and The Ulster Museum. They also had a visit to their classroom from an expert with live birds of prey. All of these first-hand kinaesthetic experiences added greatly to their learning and enthusiasm for the topic. An example of such an event is shown in Figure 8.1. The children began to ask more challenging questions and really began to study birds' wings, feathers and flight in detail. Each child became interested in a particular bird species, researched that species and shared their new information with all of us.

I also became interested in learning more about flight and the children got great pleasure in surprising me and teaching me new things, including introducing me to the cassowary bird. A number of events from this stage should be highlighted. On seeing a stuffed bald eagle in the museum, the children wanted to find out more about it. When they discovered its wing-span was two and half metres, I challenged them to make a bald-eagle with the correct wing-span to display in the school corridor. I was tempted to help them as I watched them struggle together over the measurements, but after three attempts they were successful. It was worth

FIGURE 8.1 There was great excitement and an outpouring of questions when the children met an owl

the wait to see their faces shine with such a sense of achievement and to have the satisfaction that this experience was a lesson well learnt. Too often, in the past, I would have jumped in and taken over, in frustration about precious time lost or that it was asking too much of them. Another highlight was when I introduced the class to the chirping bird toys, as they were deaf I thought the sounds of birds would not interest them, but this was not the case. The class were interested to know that birds made different sounds and some of them could distinguish that the calls were different. They listened hard and some tried to imitate by copying the teacher making the bird sounds.

By stage 2, 'Development', the children were beginning to take a real pride in their sketch books, insisting all visitors had to inspect them; photos of visits, diagrams, information, drawings and investigations were all recorded in their books. This stage really began to stretch the children and their knowledge and understanding of flight went to the next level as they investigated how birds' wings work and how similar their bone structure is to that of a human arm. They were fascinated by this and how flight patterns change according to shape and bends placed on the birds' tails or wings. This was discovered through experience, along with the meaning of 'fair-testing', 'prototypes', acting like a real scientist, and having to adapt and change plans like Leonardo da Vinci.

I read the story of Icarus to the pupils and his desire to fly rang true for many of the pupils. So the next challenge was to make wings that they could wear and then like Icarus, try them out for flight. The children had so much fun with this as they tried their best to get their bodies off the ground. Again this generated scientific questions on why they couldn't fly.

During the second stage, we also visited a Wildfowl and Wetland Trust Centre at Castle Espie. I gave the digital camera to a few of the pupils to take photos of their choice. Much to my delight, on returning to school I discovered three of the pupils had made a documentary using the video facility on the camera. I was so impressed that they had taken the initiative themselves and in watching the documentary their enthusiasm was captured. This footage subsequently appeared on Teachers TV as an example of creative practice presented by Mick Waters (Waters 2009).

In stage 3, 'Creation', the group of pupils were set the task of creating an imaginary flying creature. This provided an opportunity to allow the class to call upon all the knowledge and understanding they had developed over the past months. I asked them to each draw an imaginary bird and to label its parts and think about its habitat. The children did not copy each other, but when the drawings were compared, each had a resemblance to a cassowary (I guess it had caught their imagination). The lovely thing about The Leonardo Effect approach was that it was not competitive and every child found success at his/her own level. Together they selected their best ideas to create a working plan, with labels, which would assist them in creating the bird. This process turned out to be more complex than I had anticipated. It held lots of scientific and technological challenges. For example, selecting appropriate materials and components that would work together for making joints. Because I wanted them to think the solution out for themselves, this proved more difficult for the children, as normally I would step in to provide the answer. They called their finished bird 'Disco Mama' and it definitely proved that these children had a creative imagination.

'Disco Mama Bird' was over two metres high and was held together like a giant puppet from the ceiling. Her stomach was a disco with lights and music for her chicks to live in and enjoy. Disco Mama had a striking face and spiky boots to kick anyone who came near her young. The children were very proud of their finished bird, which was put on display for parents, pupils and staff to enjoy.

Stage 4, 'Extension', was a natural progression that allowed other aspects of the curriculum to be explored, in our case literacy. The children were able to transfer their knowledge to help them create two story books to give to the Key Stage 1 pupils. We were also involved in a visual arts competition and the pupils again used their knowledge about birds to help design costumes and a story entitled 'King of the Birds'. Of course, the drama had a bald eagle and a cassowary bird!

The Leonardo Effect was such an eye-opener for the pupils as well as myself. I discovered that giving the children more time to think and make mistakes made them better learners and was developing life-long tools for learning. The pupils' concentration, collaborative skills and close attention to detail improved dramatically, but the greatest benefit to these children was the growth in their confidence and their personal sense of achievement. Personally, I also gained so much, enjoying a more relaxed approach with time to observe their behaviour and thought processes. I now have a greater appreciation of the commonalities between Art and Science and I am hopefully a better teacher for the experience.

The Leonardo Effect with visually impaired children

As stated by Hepburn (2008), 'The Leonardo Effect' is not just about science and art. It is about facilitating cooperative learning in classrooms; about the value of out-of-school personnel (particularly experts and enthusiasts); about empowering autonomous learners; and (above all) about making connections across the 'learning landscape'. Enabling children to make connections across the curriculum is essential when teaching visually impaired children. Teaching in cross-curricular themes with a lot of hands-on concrete experiences was always our way of bringing subjects to our children rather than bringing the children to the subject.

Involvement in The Leonardo Effect pilot was particularly appealing, as art and science are important but often challenging subjects for blind and visually impaired pupils, because of the overwhelming emphasis on the visual. However, people who have lost their vision or have partial vision include famous artists, such as Claude Monet and Edgar Degas. The appeal of The Leonardo Effect also lay in the fact that the pupils would 'lead' the learning. I felt this would be the biggest challenge for our pupils because visual impairments change the way children obtain information about the world in which they grow and function, and limit opportunities to learn through observation of visual elements in the school curriculum and the people around them. There are two main functional categories of visual impairments: low vision and blind. Low-vision students usually are print users, but may require special equipment and materials. The definition of legal blindness covers a broad spectrum of visual impairments. The extent of visual disability depends upon the physical sensory impairment of the student's eyes, the age of the student at the onset of vision impairment, and the way in which that impairment occurred. Vision also may fluctuate or may be influenced by factors such as inappropriate lighting, light glare, or fatigue. Hence, there is no 'typical' vision-impaired student. Individual considerations are very important in teaching of all curricular areas to a pupil with a visual impairment. Our pupils often become reliant on others to 'lead' them and so I was keen to see if they could take ownership of *their* Flight project.

After a brainstorming session, our class decided on mechanical flight, although we joined the other class on trips, learning about natural flight. We utilised first-hand experiences in the early stages of gathering information and developing ideas. All visually impaired children need to have plenty of concrete experience, activity and reinforcement. We got plenty of this when we were able to climb inside a fuselage being constructed at the Bombardier Aircraft factory, sit at the controls of a helicopter, pace the length of an airplane at the airport, and belt up in an aircraft seat at the 'Flight Experience', to name a few of the wonderful 'hands on' experiences.

Many things that sighted people know, blind and partially sighted people can only come to know by using their remaining senses and past experiences. In the absence or limitation of sight, understanding the world is often through tactile exploration. The hands of a blind child are often called their 'eyes' because through touch they gain more useful information about their immediate environment. The tactile sense is more important for survival than the other sensory systems. Learning by touch does have distinct limitations since direct contact is necessary to perceive shape, size, texture, temperature and other qualities. Thus many objects are inaccessible because they are too far away (birds in the sky), too large (aeroplanes), too small (a ladybird), too fragile (a butterfly) or cannot even be touched (a wasp). However, the importance of interaction with real, live objects cannot be minimised. Touch senses do convey not only spatial form, but also surface quality, texture, resilience, temperature, weight and pliability, thus in many different ways going beyond impressions, resulting from visual observations. We had so many opportunities for hands-on experiences in our 'Flight' topic. For example, during our visit to Castle Espie our pupils were allowed to actively feel, handle and, when appropriate, smell, real birds' wings, beaks and feet. We got to feed the ducks and geese as they pecked food from the children's hands. A visually impaired child may not see a duck in a pond or a bird in flight, so to have these 'real' birds up close and accessible was a wonderful learning experience. At the animal sanctuary they had an owl perch on their hands or shoulders; when birds of prey were brought in to school they got to stroke a very large eagle and feel the air movement as the large bird flew over their heads. They had a go at 'flying' themselves using wings made by the other class. What a lot of fun that was! An example of this is shown in Figure 8.2.

All manipulative skills are also very important to our visually impaired children. There are several methodologies used in making art with people who are blind or visually impaired. People who are completely blind often choose three-dimensional modalities, such as clay or papier-mâché, or raised line drawing boards. Hence we made clay ducks; we also built a model airport for wooden aeroplanes, made and flew kites and helicopters.

Our creation of a mythical creature gave the perfect opportunity for cooperative learning, creative thinking skills and developing language skills, since the pupils were keen to bring together their findings. Although our imaginary creature ended up nothing like the original plan, it was founded on the accumulated knowledge the children had gained for themselves. So it had large webbed feet, the body of an aeroplane, helicopter blade antennae and many 'added-as-we-went-along features'. This ungainly creature inspired a myriad of literary activities, both written and oral. We wrote stories about where it lived, who it lived with and what it did at weekends, its likes and dislikes etc. The children were so motivated that we even created a musical drama centred around our creature with the assistance of the DRAKE Music Project. The Drake Music Project in Northern Ireland (www.drakemusic.org) exists to enable people with disabilities to compose and perform music using music technology. We ended up with a very colourful composition!

FIGURE 8.2 Experience through active participation is crucially relevant to learning and fun too

For our pupils, taking part in The Leonardo Effect pilot was a great opportunity to work independently and creatively on their own terms. The practical nature of the approach made each child equal and gave each child an opportunity to share ideas no matter what their level of vision or ability was. Moreover, the abundance of sensory experiences served to enthuse and motivate our pupils and enabled them to make connections. This was a recipe for successful learning for all involved.

References

Hepburn, H. (2008) 'The Leonardo effect takes flight', *TESS*, 25 January 2008. Online. Available at: http://www.tes.co.uk/article.aspx?storycode=2571081 (accessed 17 April 2012).

McDonald Connor, C., Hieber, S., Arts, H.A. and Zwolan, T.A. (2000) 'Speech, vocabulary, and the education of children, using cochlear implants: oral or total communication?', *Journal of Speech, Language, and Hearing Research* 43, 1185–1204.

Waters, M. (2009) 'Inspired learning video clips', Teachers Media. Online. Available at: http://www.teachersmedia.co.uk/videos/inspired-learning-video-clips-part-1 (accessed 19 April 2012).

CHAPTER

9

A Head Teacher Reflects

Fiona Loudon

Crookfur Primary is situated in Newton Mearns, in East Renfrewshire, Scotland. The school has 320 pupils, with two classes at each stage of the school. In Crookfur Primary, the aim is to provide a happy, safe environment, where all pupils are encouraged and helped to realise their potential. We foster a positive attitude to work and achievement and encourage pupils to be independent and motivated to learn, by providing high-quality learning experiences.

Following initial consultation, *A Curriculum for Excellence* was launched in Scotland in November 2004 (Scottish Government 2004). This brought a genuine feeling of excitement to education, where teachers were both enthusiastic and apprehensive about the challenges that lay ahead. The challenge for staff was to extend their current practice and take account of the totality of children's learning experiences. Effective learning and teaching are central to *A Curriculum for Excellence* and the challenge for all staff was to realise excellence in their approach: an approach that demanded more emphasis on active learning with a focus on outcomes achieved by children rather than 'inputs'. The pupils and staff at Crookfur Primary School in Primary 5 who took part in The Leonardo Effect pilot refreshed the whole school by developing ideas that helped make learning more active, challenging and enjoyable. The Leonardo Effect helped us to focus more on the 'how' of classroom practice to support learning, promote confidence, participation and responsibility. The varied and imaginative opportunities given to children to use newly acquired skills increased their motivation, which is essential to real and lasting learning.

Following the Curriculum Review Group publication in 2004, our school became involved in discussion about the integration of subjects and the promotion of transferable skills. Initial discussions around the values and principles of *A Curriculum for Excellence* (CfE) made it clear that altering the curriculum alone would not deliver the intended outcomes. It was evident that teachers needed exemplars and support in developing the necessary ethos to teach in this radical way. The four-stage methodology of The Leonardo Effect exceeded all expectations in providing that exemplar.

In Crookfur we felt restricted by topic outlines and detailed planners; although pupils were developing appropriate skills, we were not providing sufficient opportunities to promote high aspirations and ambition. 'Each child has an enormous capacity for learning and the potential to achieve in different ways' (Scottish Government 2004: 9).

As Head Teacher of Crookfur, I was excited about our involvement in the pilot from the outset, because it was a move away from prescriptive teaching and was beginning to address the values and principles of CfE. The pilot was an innovative, synchronised, integrated approach where pupils were given opportunities to research, observe, record, experiment, develop ideas, imagine and create. The approach went beyond the conventional concept of cross-curricular teaching, by utilising the commonalities of both subjects, to enrich learning and equip children to approach science confidently and more creatively. I particularly liked the idea of integrating only two subject areas, because I did not want to go back to the idea of a traditional topic web, where unnatural connections were made across subject boundaries. The Leonardo Effect is a teaching methodology that has the integration of subjects and the development of pupils' skills at its core.

The four-stage methodology of Observation and Gathering Information, Developing Ideas, Creation and Extension was an excellent approach that provided opportunities for pupils to have high aspirations and ambition. The first stage enabled pupils to direct their own learning: a visit to the Royal Society for the Protection of Birds centre at Lochwinnoch developed curiosity at the outset, with an open-ended question, 'How is flight possible?' Pupils were given opportunities to develop their ideas in the second stage, where there was an emphasis on open-ended exploration and hands-on experimentation. Specialist partners allowed pupils to develop their expertise across many areas, including making kites and investigating forces involved in flight. Within the developing ideas stage, learning was more focused, addressing particular aspects of the topic: essentially this was a practical and investigative phase, which helped to develop knowledge and build understanding. Children were given opportunities to apply their knowledge and problem-solving skills in the invention and construction of imaginary flying creatures in stage 3. Finally, they were given opportunities in stage 4 to incorporate their flying creatures into stories, drama, animation and storyboard activities, allowing for the embedding of knowledge and extension of thinking in the making of new connections.

The approach brought together the commonalities of art and science at curricular level within the same lesson. This was synchronised integration of subjects, in a stimulating, innovative and enjoyable manner. We found that it produced lasting results in children's attitudes towards the world they will ultimately contribute to. One of the key features of this process was the identification and use of joint learning outcomes by teachers. These joint learning outcomes accentuated the natural interconnectivity of art and science. The CfE document *Progress and proposals* states: 'The most important goal for science education is to stimulate, nurture and sustain the curiosity, wonder and questioning of young people' (Scottish Government 2006: 29).

In Crookfur we taught science well; however, we were uncomfortable in defending our 5–14 skills-based programme as we engaged with CfE. The 5–14 guidelines had developed into a fairly prescriptive curriculum with very little personalisation and choice. Pupils were given limited opportunities to deepen their learning and some aspects lacked breadth and challenge. The Leonardo Effect goes a long way towards ensuring our pupils find their learning challenging, engaging and motivating.

Progression was a key element of The Leonardo Effect experience because it built on previous learning in art and science. In Crookfur, Primary 1 and Primary 4 children learn about living things and forces. In art they follow a programme of study, which teaches the art skills. By Primary 5, the children had achieved basic skills, such as scientific report writing, list making, skimming and scanning, writing instructions, and had used a variety of art media. This had all been taught explicitly in previous lessons. Through The Leonardo Effect the children were then given implicit and explicit opportunities to use their own learning. The children made connections between biological and mechanical flight as well as between the subjects themselves. They progressed beyond seeing the subjects as separate entities and combined their skills to produce a flying creature, which showed a dynamic use of their skills and deeper level of understanding and curriculum coherence.

As there were no parameters to the learning, children had more choice and control over what they chose to research. The skills, knowledge and attributes to be attained in the topic had been identified, but the children greatly exceeded all expectations, including those who do not normally shine. As planning was not prescriptive and teacher-led, the children were free to explore the areas that captured their imagination and develop their creative skills.

The approach to the topic enabled teachers to match learning activities to the needs of groups and individuals, because planning was done with the children as opposed to in isolation. Opportunities were planned to develop learners' abilities to be curious and creative and to think critically.

Since the pupils were involved in determining the direction of the pilot, the class teacher's role was more of a facilitator who could provide support and challenge to enable all learners to maximise their progress. Pupils were instrumental in determining the pace of learning and many took the opportunity to research things much further than would have been expected. Open-ended tasks and activities were set that encouraged them to lead the learning and work at their own level. Learners' needs were consistently evaluated, which meant that plenary/feedback sessions were crucial in promoting next steps in learning.

A stimulating learning climate evolved in the classroom throughout the pilot and there was a consistent buzz of active learning where learners were being encouraged to think for themselves. Walking into the class was always a pleasure where pupils were consistently engaged in their learning. Learners genuinely took responsibility for aspects of their own learning and children were able to explore the areas that captured their imagination and to develop their creative skills.

Teaching fully involved learners and encouraged them to express views and ask questions. Class teachers were able to value, encourage and build upon learners' responses. Within the classroom there were excellent opportunities for active learning and the teacher–pupil interaction formed judgements of how activities met learners' needs. Support and challenge was key to the choice of tasks and activities.

An HMIE inspection of the school at the mid-point of the pilot provided a further challenge to staff in the school. There were initial concerns from staff involved because it was new to them and, although motivated by the new approach, there was apprehension about how inspectors would react. Having pupils lead their own learning is one thing, but involve an inspection in the mix and tensions can rise! When the inspection team visited Primary 5 one afternoon, they were 'blown away' by the rich variety of learning experiences, stating in their final report: 'Pupils at P5 benefited from the linking of science and art through the "Leonardo Effect" project. Pupils were leading their own learning through this stimulating context' (HM Inspectorate of Education 2007: 5).

The inspection team were impressed by the way in which pupils worked cooperatively across a range of activities. Pupils spoke with confidence about how much they had learned and had a clear direction of where they wanted to take their learning. This positive experience reaffirmed our belief that The Leonardo Effect really did work and was definitely in line with the principles and values of CfE.

Parents regularly commented about the enthusiasm their children had for the pilot. Pupils were eager to complete homework and often did work far beyond what was expected of them. They had a thirst for learning and brought research booklets and models from home that they had worked on.

As the pilot unfolded I was increasingly excited by the approach and determined that the legacy of The Leonardo Effect would live on in Crookfur. I wanted to consider the implications of CfE in terms of improving performance and further develop approaches to learning and teaching.

All the members of staff were keen to find out how they could develop The Leonardo Effect in their own classrooms and it was a key feature of the school improvement plan. A working group was established and members took responsibility for developing a synchronised art/science topic for their stage of the school. It was evident that training for teachers would be crucial for this new approach to be successful, and members of staff involved in the initial pilot led training sessions for the whole school.

The approach required a more flexible and creative approach to planning and staff had more autonomy; as head teacher I had to be confident and trust staff to ensure pupils would continue to make appropriate progress with their learning. The working group was challenged to carry out a mapping exercise of The Leonardo Effect by using the 5–14 skills of art and science and the new CfE Experiences and Outcomes. Learning and Teaching Scotland (now Education

Scotland) funded this exercise, recognising the valuable information it could provide to other practitioners. This provided an excellent opportunity for staff to think and discuss with each other about how things should be taught as much as what should be taught. Using the familiar science framework for planning, the identified science and art learning outcomes, and the four-stage methodology, teachers developed the approach using different contexts. Other topics included the over-arching questions: 'What is a minibeast?' 'How do animals move?' and 'How do planets travel?' The framework of observation and gathering information, developing ideas, creation and extension has subsequently been used to develop social subject topics using the CfE experiences and outcomes, such as: 'The Rainforest', 'The Victorians' and 'Glasgow'.

Partnership working was a key feature of the initial pilot and one that lives on in Crookfur today. As stated above, pupils started the topic by a visit to the Royal Society for the Protection of Birds centre at Lochwinnoch, which created immediate enthusiasm and a genuine desire to learn more. Other visits throughout the topic and specialists visiting the class contributed to the development of pupils' skills in a real context. Although outings can be expensive, we have continued to place a lot of value on using expertise in and out of the classroom environment. This has evolved over time and almost all topics begin with a visit out of school or a visiting specialist coming in. This has allowed us to build positive relationships with a wide variety of partners, developing pupils' skills for life, learning and work.

Throughout all topics we deliberately did not lose sight of the skills we wanted to teach. Indeed, class teachers reported that having taught the discrete skills in the first instance, they were able to develop them further and relate to real contexts.

The legacy of 'Leonardo' has lived on in Crookfur, not only through subsequent topics but in changing approaches to learning and teaching. We have continued to develop pupils' cooperative learning skills through explicit teaching, which are then practised within a context. Pupils are regularly given opportunities to lead their own learning: all teachers have seen the power this has on pupils' attainment and achievement. In Crookfur we were privileged to be part of The Leonardo Effect pilot and it has been instrumental in shaping the learning experiences of all our pupils!

References

HM Inspectorate of Education (2007) *Report on Crookfur Primary School*. Online. Available at: http://www.hmie.gov.uk/documents/inspection/8601127CrookfurPrimarySch.pdf (accessed 15 April 2012).

Scottish Government (2004) *A Curriculum for Excellence – The Curriculum Review Group*. Online. Available at: http://www.scotland.gov.uk/publications/2004/11/20178/45862 (accessed 15 April 2012).

Scottish Government (2006) *Curriculum for Excellence: Progress and proposals*. Online. Available at: http://www.scotland.gov.uk/Publications/2006/03/22090015/0 (accessed 15 April 2012).

10

Walking the Earth with our Eyes Turned Skyward

Emer Vance and Scott Vance

Leonardo da Vinci felt that there were three classes of people: those who see, those who see when they are shown and those who do not see. As a school that experiences socio-economic disadvantage, we feel that the majority of our pupils fall into the middle category. Sometimes they just need a little extra help and encouragement so that they can aspire to become 'those who see'. We are situated in a disadvantaged, urban, primary school, south of Dublin. It has a DEIS (Delivering Equality of Opportunity in Schools) Band 1 status. This means that it is listed as being in the top 300 most disadvantaged schools in the Republic of Ireland. It has eighty pupils and seven teachers comprised of five mainstream, one learning support and one special needs teacher.

When we were first approached about participating in The Leonardo Effect pilot, we were very excited and most definitely intrigued. While many of the teachers in the school taught thematically, integration between science and art wasn't always evident. Teachers felt that it was easier to establish links between subjects such as history, geography, English, art, drama and music. SESE (Social, Environmental and Scientific Education) is presented under three subject headings: history, geography and science, in the Irish Primary School Curriculum (Government of Ireland 1999). As a direct result of this, integration between these three subjects tended to be more apparent in our classroom teaching. It wasn't that teachers felt that links couldn't be made between science and art; it was more that this was an area that had not been given much attention. Thus, when given an initial outline of the methodology, we were encouraged and excited to explore both curriculums to see how they could be integrated. Similarities were immediately obvious in terms of the skills and concepts used in both subjects. While science requires pupils to observe and investigate, art encourages them to look and respond. Both require the pupils to solve problems and notice patterns, colour and texture etc. However, while the teachers felt quite excited by this new venture, they were a little daunted by and perhaps sceptical about the lack of planning required to adhere to the guidelines of the approach. In teacher training college, we are taught about the importance of planning and are conditioned to plan meticulously. Thus, preparing for an open learning approach proved to be much more complicated than planning for traditional teacher-led learning. There were fears that the children would not be motivated enough to progress with their learning, as well as concerns for classroom management and student behaviour. As such, the pilot required us to take a leap of faith. We had to examine the curriculum objectives in great detail in order to generate a series of joint learning outcomes. These became clearer as the study of 'Flight' began. The more comfortable the teachers felt with this objective, the more the approach was embraced.

While some children are naturally enthusiastic about learning, many rely heavily on the teacher to stimulate, challenge and encourage them. In addition, our teachers find that even when the pupils are actually stimulated, it is another job entirely to maintain their interest. Thus, it is the teacher's responsibility to provide topics of interest, convey to the children a perception of the topic's usefulness, instil a general desire in the pupils to achieve and, furthermore, encourage their self-confidence. In addition to this, the teacher must display endless amounts of patience, tolerance and perseverance. As I'm sure fellow educators would agree, this is a job that is much easier said than done. Before implementing The Leonardo Effect, we would have found that our pupils instinctively liked investigating science, sometimes because of their innate curiosity, but more often as a result of the hands-on nature of science and the fact that it is not literacy based. Likewise, for similar reasons, our pupils tended to enjoy the relaxed nature and the creativity of the art classroom. Since the children were used to being stimulated by the teacher, there were concerns among the staff that the approach could stall if pupils were not sufficiently self-motivated. However, initial fears about self-motivation were put to rest upon the arrival of the fantastic books and other exciting resources provided as part of the pilot. These proved to be an excellent motivator in themselves: the pupils couldn't wait to see what had arrived in the post that day. Before the pilot had even begun, the pupils began asking questions on flight relating to the resources they were seeing. Once the work was underway, its open-ended nature allowed the pupils to steer the learning in the direction of their individual interests and thus gave them a newfound ownership over their learning. The arrival of visitors to the school as well as the out-of-school trips further served to promote and maintain self-motivation. The approach required the pupils to gather information on flight through all of the various forms of media. Although the teachers were eager to begin at this point, there was a general apprehension that the low literacy levels of our pupils could hinder the learning process. The books would only prove purposeful if the pupils had the ability and were sufficiently motivated to retrieve information from them.

Improving literacy is a main focal point of the DEIS programme, with particular emphasis given to early intervention at primary-school level (Department of Education and Science 2005: 35). According to the Department of Education and Science guidelines, pupils aged 10 and above should be at a stage where reading and comprehension skills have been developed and, as such, the child should be allowed the opportunity to 'pursue personal interests in reading' (Government of Ireland 1999: 8). The main aim of this is to encourage reading for enjoyment and not simply for education purposes. The amount of success, however, is heavily reliant on the child's intrinsic motivation and a personal desire to read, something that as previously mentioned is not always evident in our pupils. However, The Leonardo Effect worked well as lessons focused on the interest of the pupils rather than on specific content objectives. As the pupils became more involved in the topic of flight, they began asking lots of questions. While some of these could only be answered through hands-on investigations, others required the pupils to look for the answers in books. The desire to answer their questions was so great that they wanted to read. Often when they would find the answer to one question, it would lead them off on a different learning tangent. Another fantastic aspect of the methodology was that it readily allowed for differentiation among the pupils with regards to literacy. Learners of all abilities were able to work at their own pace. This is extremely important, as diversity is crucial when teaching literacy to pupils if we are to build on the child's self esteem. We found that pupils who obtained lower academic achievement levels were given an equal opportunity to shine as much as their academically gifted peers. The knowledge that was being learned was seen to be transferable between both the learning support and mainstream settings.

For weeks we had been watching a group of seagulls that sat on the roof of the school. There always appeared to be one that looked as if it had only one leg. Both the pupils and I were amazed that the same seagull would keep returning to visit and one of the pupils had even named him 'Freddie'. It was some weeks later before a pupil in the learning support class saw a book on seagulls and asked if he could read it for homework. The following day, he was delighted to inform us all that seagulls actually tuck one leg up underneath their body to keep them warm, thus, more than likely, it was a different seagull that we were observing each time. The pupils' education on flight, regardless of their educational ability, was flexible, imaginative and enthused by all.

The social nature of the approach developed the pupils' skills to use literacy in a more creative, enjoyable and productive manner, as well as improving their listening and oral language skills. Pupils could be regularly overheard telling stories about things that they had noticed about flight on their way to school. One particular story comes to mind where two 10-year-old boys were discussing the pigeons they had seen near the seafront. They were describing how they moved when walking on the ground and also how tame they were. Another pupil joined in the conversation, recalling how his uncle had told him that you could train pigeons so that they would always know their way back home. I had asked them if they had noticed anything about the way the pigeons flew or landed. They said they hadn't, but that they would be going down to the seafront after school and would bring their sketch pads (an essential tool in the approach) and observe them there. The next day, as well as being greeted by a classroom full of pupils, I noticed that we had a surprise visitor, a pigeon poking its head out of a shoebox!

When asked why there was a pigeon in the classroom, the two pupils from the previous day excitedly told me that they had captured the pigeon and were going to train it to be a homing pigeon and that way they could watch it fly on a regular basis. While I greatly admired their enthusiasm and passionate involvement in the project, I gently explained that it wouldn't be very fair to the pigeon if we kept it. The pupils decided that they would like to learn more about pigeons, so a group of four boys set about researching these birds in books and on the internet. Another boy decided that he was going to interview his uncle about them, as he regarded him as a bit of a 'pigeon expert'. Although a little disappointed, the pupils who had captured the pigeon agreed that we could set it free that day. Later that morning, armed with their sketchpads and observation notebooks, the class gazed at the pigeon as it flew away and landed on the top of the water tower beside the school. Although the whole event may not have complied fully with animal welfare regulations, the pupils learned a few valuable lessons about flight as well as on the safety of wildlife.

Overall, our teachers noticed how the children wanted to talk about flight in its various forms, whether it was in relation to what they were working on in class, things that they had noticed after school or documentaries that they had watched on television. All of our teachers felt that literacy levels in general improved across the board. The pupils' use of vocabulary expanded in both their oral and written work as words associated with flight became imprinted in their minds.

Another unexpected observation was the huge improvement in pupils with behavioural problems. One pupil in particular comes to mind who was always in trouble, both in the playground and in class. He had a mild general learning disability and was prone to hyperactivity. He became completely engrossed from the very beginning. Instead of trying to disrupt others, he took on the role of leader in his group. He couldn't wait for the afternoon to come when he could continue his work on flight. Two afternoons a week he had to attend the learning support class for half an hour. I remember clearly on one occasion this pupil bursting through the door after his learning support session asking what he had missed. He would delve straight into his work, whether it was researching information in a book, sketching a design or working on his flying creature. It was agreed soon after the commencement of the pilot that it would be more beneficial for this pupil if the learning support teacher came into the mainstream class to help with the work, rather than removing him from a setting where he was performing well and making great gains in terms of his education. His relationship with both his peers and myself improved greatly throughout the pilot because many of our goals and aspirations for success were in harmony with each other.

Another positive outcome was the impact The Leonardo Effect had on parental involvement with the school. As a school with disadvantaged status, we often find it quite difficult to get parents actively involved in their children's education. While our parents undoubtedly care for their children, they can sometimes find it difficult to understand the importance of education. Often this stems from their own educational experience. Other times, emotional problems, learning difficulties, lack of time or simply the fact that they may feel lacking in knowledge can prevent them from becoming involved. Throughout the various phases of the pilot, the pupils were going home very excited about what they were doing and learning in school. Parents would tell us how their children would point out things to do with flight as they were out walking. Something as simple as how, all of a sudden, a leaf would fall from a tree became interesting. The children began noticing detail such as the veins in the leaves, their overall shape and how these factors influenced the way they fell. This sense of excitement and eagerness to learn encouraged parents to take notice and focus on their child's learning. The pupils were arriving in school recounting conversations that they had with their parents about flight. We noticed that there seemed to be a shared dialogue on flight between parents and their children. Without a doubt this form of parental involvement could only act to further support and promote school success as well as instilling a sense of pride in the child.

The Leonardo Effect was a fantastic experience for our school where success was gained by all. The pupils were captivated by the excitement, a captivation that in turn led to an increase in literacy levels, self-motivation and cooperative learning. Furthermore, the skills that were learned or improved upon were seen to be transferrable, as reading and spellings improved. Pupils became used to carrying out independent research and, as such, continued to do so with other topics when involvement in the pilot finished. Pupils with behavioural problems showed a greater interest in their learning, while parents became proud to be involved. Both teachers and the school principal felt that the methodology promoted quality learning across the curriculum, particularly in terms of art, science and literacy, but also in terms of history, geography, drama and music. Teachers also realised the importance of using the children's interests to guide and develop learning, something that was taken on board beyond the pilot. Finally, as well as inspiring and stimulating our pupils, The Leonardo Effect enabled them to independently become 'those who see'.

References

Department of Education and Science (2005) *Delivering Equality of Opportunity in School: An action plan for educational inclusion*, Dublin: Stationery Office.

Government of Ireland (1999) *Revised Primary School Curriculum. Teacher guidelines*, Dublin: Stationery Office.

11

Synchronised Integration of Art and Science: A Model for Excellence in the Scottish Primary Classroom

Jem Anderson

Like the great Leonardo himself, the pupils in Primary 5 at Crookfur Primary School became both artists and scientists who took control of their own learning and used their newfound knowledge to fuel their imaginations. The facilitators/teachers in the process were Nancy Neil and me. Unlike the great Leonardo, we were neither artists nor scientists of great distinction. Nancy, however, was a very skilful teacher with over 30 years' teaching experience and at the time I was embarking on my second year of teaching, with all the spark a new teacher brings. Crookfur is semi open plan, so this meant the two very lively Primary 5 classes, a total of 62 children, were doing the pilot together. Nancy and I would team teach, steering the pupils towards answering 'How is Flight Possible?' over a 12-week period.

Importantly, we were given the freedom and trust by our management team to deliver The Leonardo Effect. Our line manager accompanied us on the initial training days and therefore had a first-hand understanding of the aims of the approach and grasped the need to have confidence in Nancy and me to deliver it. She was as enthused and committed as we were. However, perhaps even more importantly we were provided with the necessary curriculum flexibility and structural support to deliver it effectively. Our head teacher provided us with the non-class contact time needed to think through and put in place the methodology effectively. We used this time to match the learning outcomes of the approach to the existing 5–14 guidelines and the emerging new Scottish Curriculum entitled *Curriculum for Excellence* (CfE). We identified the key skills we knew pupils had to acquire. We organised resources, trips and visiting experts. Through discussion and reading, we 'got our heads around' The Leonardo Effect.

Having absorbed the stages of The Leonardo Effect into our thinking, we knew that the first stage 'Gathering Information' was where learning should come from, a first-hand experience of the world, from a need to know. We began in January at the Lochwinnoch RSPB centre. It was what we call in Scotland a *dreich* day – miserable. But rather than being stuck in a classroom on their second day back at school, our pupils were off on an unlikely adventure into the great outdoors and it completely captured their interest. All the children without exception were engaged. They were armed with cameras, and being able to take photographs of what caught their eye was highly motivating.

The next day we had a follow-up discussion to gather the information gained and we were astounded by how much they had learned. Some pupils gave us an explanation for the differences in male and female feather colour, whilst others described the wing adaptations of owls as opposed to eagles. It was clear to us that field trips, which had hitherto been a celebration at the end of a topic, could be purposeful learning experiences and a crucial springboard to develop our learning at the beginning of a topic.

We had heard at the training event that The Leonardo Effect would provide an 'irresistible context' for literacy. This was certainly true for our Primary 5 children, and began with detailed recounts of our trip. Because the memories were so fresh and strong in their minds, the quality of the recounts, and indeed writing, from every pupil was substantially better. Indeed, children who normally avoided writing at all costs were enjoying writing about what they had experienced.

Teachers and pupils all knew from our post-trip discussion that feathers' size, shape, colour, adaptations to habitat and purpose would be our starting point. The children would lead the learning in this way. At the end of each lesson we would discuss the key learning points from that day. The teachers would facilitate and guide the discussion, allowing the children to identify what was important to learn next. So, for example, from the trip it was feathers. Alongside this, pupils had opportunities for personalisation and choice to develop knowledge in their own areas of interest, which, it became clear, they would wholeheartedly grasp. Our able learners could explain things in scientific detail and often brought in their own books, drawings and artefacts. The pilot enabled our several able children to become 'experts' because they had much more control over the parameters of their learning. Catering for them need not be an 'add on': it was embedded in the nature of the approach.

We, the teachers, were learning alongside the pupils, only sometimes managing to keep a step ahead. This was very different from the way learning had hitherto happened in our classroom. Teachers' planners would contain a list of key teaching points that you had to cover during the teaching of a given topic. It was our job to ensure the children 'knew' these key ideas by the end of the unit of work. In contrast, we were opening up the list of important teaching points to the pupils. They were 'discovering' what was important to know, rather than being told. We learnt about the key ideas along with them, finding good websites with them, reading the books alongside them, researching Leonardo together.

The heart of the approach, the synchronised integration of art and science, meant joint learning outcomes (JLOs) for teachers. When taking a closer look at feathers, the JLO was to investigate and draw a feather. To be successful, pupils had to touch it, feel it and talk about it, paying close attention to colour, line and texture. This fulfilled both the CfE second-level art experience and outcome: 'Through observing and recording from my experiences across the curriculum, I can create images and objects which show my awareness and recognition of detail' (Scottish Executive 2009b). It also covered the CfE science overarching experience and outcome: 'Learning in the sciences will enable me to develop curiosity and understanding of the environment' (Scottish Executive 2009a).

Looking both as artists and scientists meant the children didn't look at objects as merely things to draw but as a means to understanding how a small part, a feather, could make a bigger thing work, or in this case fly.

One pupil recorded, 'Getting to feel and draw the feathers helped us to understand their colours and how light they are'.

It was clear we needn't worry that either subject would play a secondary role because the children understood their synchronised nature. Discussing the JLO at the start of each lesson or activity was vital, but The Leonardo Effect also requires a constant wider discussion about the learning journey: for us the progress towards answering 'How is Flight Possible?' Nancy and I would reflect on and discuss where each day's lessons were taking us, towards answering that overarching question.

And that was the difficult part – each day's lessons. Organising the learning was without doubt the biggest challenge we faced. However, we had support in a number of key ways. First, the training we received was dynamic, memorable and practical. We used all of the ideas we had seen and experienced there. Second, three afternoons minimum each week were devoted to The Leonardo Effect. This de-cluttering of the curriculum allowed us to plan longer stretches of learning. Thirdly, we managed to schedule the computer suite and Pupil Support Assistant for when we were doing the pilot. Lastly, as mentioned earlier, we had a very supportive management team who gave us time and advice when we needed it.

Our learning followed different formats. Sometimes all 62 pupils worked on the same thing, sometimes we worked as separate classes, but often we used the children's 'houses' to divide our 62 pupils into three or four mixed ability groups of around 15 to 20 and offered them a variety of learning experiences in the one afternoon. These activities either had the same learning outcome, reinforced by doing it in different ways, or its own specific learning outcome. We the teachers would work with a group each, whilst one group worked independently, and whenever possible the Pupil Support Assistant worked with the fourth group, supporting our pupils with Additional Support Needs.

It is worth pointing out, however, that, if you had walked into our classroom we would have made a bet you couldn't pick out the 'less able' learners. Of the 62 pupils, we had a spread of children working on Level A to D of the 5–14 Scottish Curriculum or Early to Second Level of CfE, including a high percentage with English as an Additional Language (EAL). We found over the 12 weeks that we couldn't get teaching started in the morning without children coming up to us with things they had done or found at home. One child who had Attention Deficit Hyperactivity Disorder and difficulty retaining information was remembering amazing facts. Another with Asperger's Syndrome was using his mathematical talents to work out how many times the humming bird would flap its wings in two or three hours! Because the methodology facilitated a culture of ideas and independent learning, the children weren't scared to make mistakes or contribute to the class.

By the end of our first week the learning had quickly progressed. The JLO was to identify and demonstrate how the different parts of a bird's body enable flight. One group accompanied me to carry out research in the computer suite. They were guided by a pre-prepared PowerPoint presentation, hyperlinked to relevant websites; a second group worked on one side of the classroom, taking notes from books and writing them on giant sheets of paper; the third group was watching a DVD on the interactive whiteboard, which they paused in order to draw an osprey in full flight, and the fourth group were making prints of feathers using polystyrene. Within the larger groups, children were working individually, in pairs or in small groups. For the most part we let them decide how they would like to work. The children had 20 minutes on each activity and were therefore regularly refocused, moving around, kept on task, and the classroom atmosphere was buzzing.

This excitement about learning was undoubtedly sustained by the first-hand experiences, visiting experts and variety of resources the children were able to engage with. A visit to Amazonia, Scotland's largest indoor tropical rainforest, broadened our knowledge of biological flight. This knowledge was developed further by owls from Kelburn Falconry Centre swooping into our classroom. Then getting outdoors with flying toys, such as kites, ornithopters and gyroscope helicopters, enabled pupils to engage in purposeful play, a task not normally associated with pupils in the middle years of primary education. Through discussion the toys led us to widen our research to mechanical flight. The format of class discussions was always 'mixed ability thinking partners' and 'no hands up'. Even though the children were having great fun, the focus was always on developing thinking about flight and helping each other in that collaborative process.

Collaborative learning was increasingly important for our Primary 5 pupils who naturally progressed on to the second stage 'Developing Ideas'. Pupils developed ideas from the outset; however, as we began to consider applying our learning in the construction of our imaginary flying creatures, pupils had opportunities to work in groups to investigate materials and structures. From our training we knew it was vital the children had opportunities to experiment and investigate in an open-ended way, just as Leonardo himself had done. Our skill as teachers was to observe and chat with pupils while they worked, then decide how we could enhance their technical skills and knowledge.

The children experimented with a wide range of materials, tackling challenges and solving problems, such as 'How tall can you make a newspaper structure?' 'How many ways can you join the art straws?' 'Can you keep it in the air?' 'Can you make it fly?' We then set a more structured challenge of designing, creating and evaluating a kite. Alongside this the children were taking inspiration from the Wright brothers and the discoveries they made about wing warping and triangular wing structures. This along with their learning from biological flight fed into their experimentation.

At the beginning of week seven we visited the aircraft hangar at James Watt College, where engineers explained different aspects of aeroplane construction and demonstrated the equipment. The children were able to sit inside a 30-year-old RAF plane and have their photograph taken. Not surprisingly, many of them reported a desire to become aeronautical engineers – motivation was immeasurable. Capitalising on this high, pupils received a visit from a professional artist. Using his own artwork he explained the aesthetic design principles of present and past aircraft. Based on what they had learned, the children designed their own unique symmetrical artwork for the Polikarpov, a World War Two Russian fighter aircraft.

Eight weeks after we started the pilot, the third stage of The Leonardo Effect 'Creation' was underway. Both teachers and pupils concluded that the best way to organise this stage would be to work in groups. We knew creativity would be enhanced if the class worked collaboratively to design and make imaginary flying creatures. We were also more likely to have enough materials to go around. Groups were the way forward for us. So pupils decided on specific roles they would be good at and we had a balance of those roles in each group and an agreed code for group work.

In making a prototype just before the creation stage, it was clear the children were applying their knowledge of materials and joining techniques, which would enable flight. This gave us confidence that their design briefs would be detailed and thoughtful. We were not disappointed and the children showed immense creativity, imagination, skill and knowledge in the creation of their imaginary flying creatures. The idea of a visual outcome for the knowledge they had gained was one of the most powerful aspects of The Leonardo Effect. For the pupils, being able to display their knowledge and understanding of flight, but at the same time being able to add imagination and creativity, was challenging and exciting. For the teachers it was a messy business, with giant structures and materials taking up a huge amount of space, but for only three weeks it was well worth it to see the children becoming 'Little Leonardos'.

One of the reasons our 'Little Leonardos' took such great pride in their creations was the knowledge they would be descending upon the Glasgow Science Centre alongside the flying creations of Carolside Primary School in a fantastic display of work. It was magical scene to see the prestigious Glasgow Science Centre acting as a showcase for the work of our pupils. *The Herald* and *Daily Mail* newspapers recognised the importance of The Leonardo Effect at Crookfur Primary and wrote in strong praise of the approach. 'The achievements of The Leonardo Effect initiative have not gone unnoticed. Crookfur's HMIE report picked up on the benefits to the children of "leading their own learning through this stimulating context"' (MacLarty 2007). Invitations from HMIE to speak at a 'good practice' conference and an opportunity to speak at the Scottish Learning Festival about The Leonardo Effect only served to confirm its importance.

It was clear to my head teacher that The Leonardo Effect could not be a 'one off'. It was embedded in my own and Nancy's practice and indeed the curriculum of Primary 5. In the following year as I moved from Primary 5 to Primary 1, as part of whole school development of the curriculum, I applied The Leonardo Effect methodology where I posed the question 'How do insects fly?' with very young children. Open-ended, investigative and explorative learning was already a key feature of our infant department, where the Head of the Infant Department led the successful implementation of purposeful play and active learning. The introduction of The Leonardo Effect sat well with the existing learning ethos.

Having taught Primary 1 in my probationary year, I knew the science topic of living things could be developed in more depth. Posing the question 'How do insects fly?' was a natural progression of pupils' existing knowledge and would build on skills gained in previous topics. Working with my Primary 1 colleague, we did not have the same budget for trips and visiting specialists, but we did manage to capture their imagination with a visit to the Edinburgh Butterfly Kingdom and in other inventive and inexpensive ways: we had caterpillars in the classroom and documented their change into butterflies; we turned the library into a bat cave with books all about flight and stocked the writing table with a variety of flying insect-themed stimuli; we observed a dead bee under a digital microscope linked to the interactive whiteboard; we made model dragonflies and 3D junk model butterflies.

For assessment purposes I videoed the children making their 3D junk model butterflies. As they worked, they could explain in great detail the anatomy of the butterfly and the purpose each body part served. They were able to discuss size, shape and proportions of the three different insects we had studied. They were experts on camouflage and its purpose. When I shared the work of the topic with other Primary 1 teachers at East Renfrewshire Council's Early Years Forum, they were amazed by the standard of the written work the children achieved. In particular, the non-chronological reports the children had written about butterflies were the subject of a few gasps.

> The thorax is where the wings are attached [to the butterfly] and it pushes the food down into the abdomen with its muscles.

> (Pupil aged 6)

The Primary 1 project culminated in the creation of our imaginary flying insect the 'Caviramdo Butterfly'. In pairs and small groups, the children were set the challenge of designing an imaginary flying insect. As a class, they examined all the designs and had a secret ballot to vote for their favourite. They then divided into groups responsible for the production of different parts and listed all the materials they would need before they set to work building and then assembling the Caviramdo. They evaluated the finished model against the design brief and agreed for the most part they had stuck to the plan. The children then wrote imaginative stories about the Caviramdo, where it had different flying adventures depending on who the Primary 1 author was. It was evident again in Primary 1 that The Leonardo Effect provides an 'irresistible context' for literacy.

For teachers in Scotland, providing dynamic contexts for learning has never been so salient. The *Curriculum for Excellence* states that 'Learning in the sciences will enable [pupils] to recognise the role of creativity and inventiveness in the development of the sciences' (Scottish Executive 2009a: 1) and 'enable [them] to experience the inspiration and power of the arts' (Scottish Executive 2009b: 1).

The Leonardo Effect is a powerful vehicle to realise this goal. The introduction of the *Curriculum for Excellence* has given teachers in Scotland the opportunity to look at commonalities between the experiences and outcomes across curricular areas and provide a more holistic education for our pupils. This is not always an easy task, but The Leonardo Effect provides a blueprint for effective change. Planning flight in Primary 1 and Primary 5, we found several experiences and outcomes were effortlessly covered by the methodology in not only art and science but importantly literacy and numeracy and also technology. Furthermore, in looking closely at the values, purposes and principles of the *Curriculum for Excellence*, we realised they are embedded in the approach.

I feel extremely privileged to have been part of the pilot. The pedagogy I was introduced to has formed the foundations of my teaching knowledge and the methodology fundamentally changed me as a teacher, and my outlook on learning. My colleague Nancy has now hung up her teaching hat, I'm sure she will reflect back on that year in Primary 5 at Crookfur, along with the pupils and me, as one of the best. I hope I can continue to make learning inspirational and memorable as I further embed The Leonardo Effect in my classroom. I hope those of you reading this chapter will pilot The Leonardo Effect in your own classrooms and give your pupils the opportunity to be inspired artists and scientists and unleash their imaginations.

I promise you, it works.

References

MacLarty, L. (2007) 'The Light Fantastic: How schools are cracking the Da Vinci Code', *The Herald Society* 3 July. Online. Available at: http://www.leonardoeffect.com/resources/herald.pdf (accessed 20 April 2012).

Scottish Executive (2009a) *Curriculum for Excellence: Science experience and outcomes*. Online. Available at: http://www.ltscotland.org.uk/Images/sciences_experiences_outcomes_tcm4-539927.doc (accessed 21 April 2012).

Scottish Executive (2009b) *Curriculum for Excellence: Art and design experience and outcomes*. Online. Available at: http://www.ltscotland.org.uk/myexperiencesandoutcomes/expressivearts/artanddesign/index.asp (accessed 21 April 2012).

12

A Student Teacher Asks: Can The Leonardo Effect Enhance Literacy Attainment in Boys?

Helen McKernan

Debate regarding boys' under-achievement in literacy has escalated in recent years, fuelled by the increasing availability of national performance statistics. I became concerned with the issue during a previous school placement in a boys' primary school, as part of my undergraduate education degree. This motivated me to investigate the barriers to boys' literacy attainment and think about how the problem could be addressed. From my knowledge of The Leonardo Effect gained as part of my studies, I had the idea of employing this approach in a case study to see if it would provide enriched literacy opportunities that might engage boys and extend their literacy abilities. The following describes my attempts to develop a learning environment in which boys would be more motivated to develop literacy skills.

Under-achievement in boys' literacy is a pervasive theme in both public and academic debate. Within my own jurisdiction of Northern Ireland, the Northern Ireland Audit Office (2006) states that the performance of boys continues to lag significantly behind girls. A similar pattern exists across the United Kingdom. Concern stems from national statistics and Ofsted (2003) highlighting the legitimate alarm over the under-achievement of some boys' throughout their schooling. The Department for Education Northern Ireland (2007) supports this finding.

Explanations for boys' under-achievement vary depending on perspective. Ofsted (2003) claim personal factors such as motivation are some of the most pressing problems, possibly indicating to teachers the need to find ways and means to motivate reluctant pupils. Munns et al. (2006) appear to corroborate this, suggesting that knowledge of boys' behaviours and interests are crucial to developing an understanding of their motivation to learn and engage with schooling. Barrs and Pidgeon (1998, 2002) argue that classroom approaches, teaching strategies and particularly lack of engagement with texts are pressing problems for literacy achievement in boys. Teaching strategies based on text book comprehension as a means to develop literacy do not engage pupils' imaginations, nor do they facilitate sensory experience and emotional involvement; therefore creative responses to texts and ideas are limited. Reference to creativity in both teachers and pupils and developing imagination is common in relation to identifying strategies to engage boys with literacy.

In 1999 The National Advisory Committee on Creative and Cultural Education (NACCCE) claimed that creativity is a key element in developing successful readers and writers. Craft et al. (2008) support this, stating effective literacy teaching rests on teacher creativity, characterised by innovation, providing pupils with an ownership of knowledge and taking control of the teaching process, making it relevant to the learner and adding variety to literacy experiences. Buzan (2001) has a similar view: encouraging children to become creative and imaginative thinkers requires teachers to present springboards for learning, allowing pupils' curiosity to initiate opportunities for imagination, observation, emotion and sensations, so that children actually desire to have-a-go and take risks. Some teachers may find this approach difficult, if creativity is not one of their strengths, yet it appears to be an under-estimated ingredient for children's learning to flourish.

Safford et al. (2004) consider understanding of 'boy-friendly' pedagogies or learning styles to be crucial, arguing that boys tend to thrive in practical classrooms, where interactive activities and challenges are adopted as a means to acknowledge the central importance of talk. Primarily, this requires teachers to take some risks, embracing their creativity to introduce more variety to literacy, while identifying speaking and listening as means to support writing development.

Evidence is also accumulating that exposing pupils to the visual arts can strengthen and foster their literacy skills. This especially fascinates me as an undergraduate education student specialising in art. Halpern presents many possible pathways linking visual and expressive art processes with literacy education, claiming that, 'For children who have begun to struggle with literacy, re-approaching it through and incorporating it into another art form removes some of the psychological baggage that may have begun to accumulate' (2006: 35). Barrs and Pidgeon (1998) also appreciate the value of art as an instrument through which to channel meaningful literacy experiences based on visualisation. The processes of art engage pupils in discovery learning, through collecting images, observing and experiencing sensations and emotions, then discussing them in detail, noticing what the pupils could hear, see, smell or touch. This has much in common with my experience of teaching science. The Leonardo Effect, in allowing for the commonalities shared by art and science to be brought together in teaching these subjects, has numerous benefits for literacy. I know that, through The Leonardo Effect, discussing observations and realising visualisations can take many literal forms, including burst writing, word banks and frames or concept maps. It also incorporates speaking and listening grounded in real situations. There have been many instances in my teaching where spontaneous discussion has arisen among groups of children, or formal talk in presentations has been required. Such instances develop a wider view of literacy for pupils who naturally engage with it because they have something they wish to communicate.

My motivation to experiment with The Leonardo Effect as a means to improve boys' literacy attainment derives from my belief and confidence in the potential and educational value of art and design, which is synchronised with science in this approach. It is evident that some teachers' attitudes and perceptions of art can be vague or uncertain, based either on a product-driven approach or employing art as an incentive for good behaviour, both of which undermine the value of art as an adaptable and transferable subject and so it is not exploited to its full potential. Addison et al. (2003) warn that unless art education is taught effectively, its potential for strengthening literacy is considerably reduced.

The undermining of art may also be attributed to the emphasis that has been placed on numeracy and literacy within the curriculum, although the *Cambridge Primary Review* makes the recommendation to 'wind up the primary national strategy and re-integrate literacy and numeracy with the rest of the curriculum' (Alexander 2010: 511). The Leonardo Effect supports this idea, claiming that art and science can perform as genuine partners in generating enhanced teaching and learning opportunities throughout the curriculum (Robson et al. 2007).

On the basis of what I had learned of under-achievement in boy's literacy, my intention was to apply The Leonardo Effect methodology in a classroom context to see if this would build the literacy strengths of boys through empowering them to:

- take ownership of their learning;

- experience variety in literacy tasks based on integrating the visual, kinaesthetic processes within the verbal and textual environment of literacy; and

- find literacy more appealing, enjoyable and relevant.

Teaching strategy and implementation

My six-week study involved a class of nineteen pupils aged 10–11 years old: eleven boys and eight girls. Although the teaching programme was delivered to the whole class my primary focus was to monitor literacy in boys. I identified six main themes to build my teaching around.

- Pupil engagement.

- Pupil-directed learning and motivation.

- Visual learning with hands-on experiences.

- Boy-friendly pedagogies.

- Genuine integration of subjects.

- Creativity and imagination.

To enhance pupil engagement, pupil-directed learning and motivation, I employed the basic principles of The Leonardo Effect of first-hand observation, investigation and flexible planning involving children's ideas, to surmount the barriers posed to boys in developing their literacy skills. This approach corresponded to the ideas of Craft, Buzon and the NACCCE outlined above, and therefore strongly influenced my choice to plan flexibly with specific focus placed on listening to pupils' ideas and experiences. Had a preconceived scheme of work been implemented with no recognition of pupils' interests and curiosities, I fear that the children's creativity and ownership may have been stifled. According to the class teacher it revealed unrecognised abilities in some pupils, allowing them to go from strength to strength, gaining confidence and being adventurous learners. If we can give children more choice in how they learn, and explore with them the reasons why they are learning, then we will have more success in improving their motivation and engagement.

Initially we discussed a range of possible topics for pupils to select. I anticipated the boys would be interested in visiting a local mill to develop the topic of industrial machinery, or local myths and legends connected, for example, with the Giants Causeway, but it became clear that they were much more interested in the topic of fishing. They were keen to explore fish, bring in fishing rods, bait, hooks etc. Unknown to any of us at the beginning, this would later develop into the creation of mythical sea monsters. The teaching strategy concentrated on sensory first-hand experiences, encouraging children to employ their natural ability to be imaginative, to seek out areas they wished to investigate and to become partners in planning their learning. Sensory stimulus acted as a springboard for pupils' curiosity, inspiring imaginative thinking and self-generated questions.

From the start, selecting themes allowed the pupils to take ownership. This also led them into questioning and rethinking their prior knowledge. Therefore, approaching written text from different sources became a means to discover or rediscover new and different things about their topic, constantly questioning and developing their understanding. In talk teams, pupils were encouraged to share their interpretations with one another, thus discovering new and different perspectives: they were then able to return to their visual work and review it by reflecting and integrating these new discoveries.

I adopted organisational tables to record ideas, including grids, keys, writing frames and concept maps, as well as a class KWL board, however the children favoured mind-mapping as a means to record. On reviewing the mind maps, I found each one to be unique, indicating that each child had responded by using the information accrued to fill gaps that were specific to their prior understanding of the topic.

Once the class had decided on the theme of sea monsters, pupils began to gather information, blending, mixing and matching knowledge drawn from diverse textual sources, such as newspaper reports on sightings of the Loch Ness Monster, and visual media. During this process pupils surprised me one lunchtime with a mass of images of monkfish they printed from the internet. As a facilitator I found my role in aiding the children to generate ideas, offering experiences so that the pupils could use their imaginations, observations and emotions to play with possibilities, wondering what, why and how. 'Gathering Information' embraced the form of written texts. Initially we explored two books, *The Water Horse* (a story about Nessy, the Loch Ness Monster) by Dick

King-Smith (2008) and *Percy Jackson and the Sea of Monsters* by Rick Riordan (2008) for the more able readers. This led on to exploring poetry, internet sources, newspaper articles and sensory experiences with sea life.

I first approached the text utilising talk teams during guided reading. As the children read, they each prepared to play a role, for example: scene setter, word wizard or content catcher. Pupils then took part in active talking and listening, reporting their findings back to the group and discussing them. Visual and tactile experimentation embraced realistic purposes, initially with various species of fish. Pupils were encouraged to respond to and record detailed observations, ideas and information. One pupil responded to the scales of the fish, exploring various media in the attempt to recreate the pattern. I also adopted drama-based activities with specific purposes, exploring the mood, plot and setting of the text through role play, improvisations and visualisations. This prepared pupils with a visual stimulus based on factual information, which they could then integrate with fantasy during creative writing.

By giving the children the opportunity to create not only with words, but with line, colour and movement, I acknowledged the value of visual and kinaesthetic learning alongside verbal. The class teacher commented positively on the change of attitude towards talking and listening. Pupils began to comment critically and analytically regarding sources of information, rather than simply repeating or describing. Art and science seemed to act as a basis on which to build and strengthen literacy, encouraging verbal imagination sparked by visual and sensory experiences expressed first visually, then in words.

Boy-friendly pedagogies or learning styles tend to be largely interactive. Safford et al. (2004) argue that boys tend to thrive in practical classrooms where tasks or challenges are adopted as a means to acknowledge the central importance of talk. The 'Development of Ideas' stage of the work was driven by their curiosity and mainly involved multi-sensory experiences that required pupils to recall prior knowledge, to discover patterns and similarities and invest energy, realising that one idea will lead to another. Lessons took the form of print making, based on the recreation of skin texture and testing for water resistance. Process and instructional writing were used to record the materials and methods pupils used for creation. Clay modelling embraced self-expression, allowing pupils to individually interpret the characteristics of 'Nessy'. More focused investigations were carried out, depending on the pupils' interests. One group began in-depth investigation and experimentation on anatomical features such as gills, fins, scale patterns and textures, another group studied how species are adapted to live underwater. They all drew on evidence from factual sea life sources, including the National Geographic website. Other pupils invested their imagination and innovation towards fictional representations of the Loch Ness Monster, initially comprising a word bank that best described their impressions of visual characteristics.

The 'Development of Ideas' stage was exciting, with the genuine integration of subjects. Art and science offered a productive context for developing speaking and listening skills. Pupils embraced long sessions of serious, subject-based talking to think through their problems, playing with possibilities and evaluating suitability of ideas. Areas of art and science became a rich verbal as well as visual environment, contributing to the pupils' ability to express thoughts, feelings and opinions in response to personal experiences and visual media, addressing the literacy objectives defined in the Northern Ireland Curriculum (CCEA 2007). I found independent focused work to be beneficial for boys especially, as there was emphasis on talk and time to reflect. Explicit attention was paid to the creation of a secure classroom environment where mistakes were valued as learning experiences, equally important to being correct in the overall learning process. Pupils immersed themselves in visual work, receiving great satisfaction from the independent thinking this involved, setting their own aims, objectives and targets, building on previous learning and demonstrating impressive recall, interpretation and organisational skills.

When pupils felt they had accumulated adequate information, experiences, inspiration and skills, they embarked on the 'Creation' stage, planning and designing a three-dimensional sea monster, drawing on the factual, visual and technical knowledge they had acquired through the 'Gathering Information' and 'Development of Ideas' stages. The processes of creation deepened the learning experience; it required pupils to unify their imaginings with observations, emotions and sensations to invent a visual response that embodied their design plan. Design plans took the form of detailed labelled sketches and drawings. During construction, groups of pupils took responsibility for different parts of the creature. They used information from their earlier drawings, models, factual information etc., embracing the language, discussing in pairs and as a whole class, possible patterns, colours, textures and dimensions for their monster. Interaction between pupils was both verbal and non-verbal, reflecting the various thinking, talking and listening skills they developed through evaluating and testing the construction techniques.

The 'Extension Stage' was utilised to facilitate the embedding of knowledge and to make further connections based on the context of their own sea monster, consolidating learning through realistic and personal experiences. The visual design acted as a model from which to sculpt and fashion creative writing, combining story boards, burst writing, oral narratives, paired and group oral and visual presentations. This period was largely about communicating ideas, providing the children with time, space and an audience so that they could explain and evaluate their ideas, solutions and also express their enjoyment and worries.

The level of commitment and interest shown by the children by far surpassed my expectations. Ignoring the idea of a preconceived and highly organised scheme of work allowed for a more open-ended approach directed by the pupils, thus teaching and learning strategies were more diverse, creating quality learning opportunities. The learning environment was both fun and enjoyable as well as challenging and, at times, demanding. However, pupils collaborated and contributed to produce wonderful, individual work grounded on textual motivation.

Conclusions

Based on the results of my research, clear conclusions can be drawn in respect of literacy. I found that boys love working visually and enjoy the independent thinking this entails. Involving them in the sensory hands-on procedures of art and science helps them to engage, thus reaching out to boys who may have been previously uninterested or easily distracted by more prescriptive instructional methods.

Essentially art enables boys to approach literacy from another perspective, a visual one, and if, as Safford et al. (2004) claim, boys tend to draw on visual sources for their writing, then art acts as a medium for translating these visual images first verbally then in coherent written text.

The sensory first-hand experiences enable boys to employ their natural ability to be imaginative, to seek out subjects for investigation and become partners in planning their learning. Thus participation and motivation in literacy can be improved in a non-artificial way.

The synchronised integration of art and science in The Leonardo Effect can act as a vehicle on which to build and strengthen literacy, because it encourages verbal imagination sparked by visual and sensory experiences expressed first visually then in words. In addition, boys found the synchronised integration of the two subjects more attractive than taking a single subject-based approach. This manifested in a desire by the boys to become engaged in reading and communication about the areas of study that they saw had relevance and value.

Visual work such as three-dimensional work in clay, experiments in texture, textiles and photography can act as models from which to sculpt and fashion creative writing, story boards, burst writing, oral narratives, paired and group oral and visual presentations. Merging literacy with art and science presents the possibility of broadening the writing experience in terms of preparation and exploration, allowing children to lead from their strengths, to gain confidence and risk take. Throughout this case study, flexible planning established a methodology that empowered pupils to take control of the learning process, making it more relevant and engaging. More important, it was clear that it made literacy more appealing, enjoyable and relevant to boys, regardless of their level of ability, all of which have been identified as requirements for improving literacy attainment in boys.

References

Addison, A., Burgess, P. and Freedman, K. (2003) *Issues in Art and Design Teaching*, London: Routledge Falmer.

Alexander, R.J. (ed.) (2010) *Children, their World, their Education. Final report and recommendations of the Cambridge Primary Review*. London: Routledge.

Barrs, M. and Pidgeon, S. (1998) *Boys and Reading*, Southwark: Centre for Language in Primary Education.

Barrs, M. and Pidgeon, S. (eds) (2002) *Boys and Writing*, London: Centre for Language in Primary Education.

Buzan, T. (2001) *The Power of Creative Intelligence*, London: Harper Collins.

CCEA (2007) *The Northern Ireland Curriculum*, Belfast: Council for the Curriculum, Examinations and Assessment.

Craft, A., Gardner, H. and Claxton, G. (2008) *Creativity, Wisdom and Trusteeship: Exploring the role of education*, London: SAGE.

Department for Education Northern Ireland (2007) *Literacy and Numeracy of Pupils in Northern Ireland*, Bangor: Department for Education Northern Ireland.

Halpern, R. (2006) 'Critical issues in after-school programming', in F. Stott (ed.) *Mono graph of the Herr Research Center for Children and Social Policy*, Chicago: Erikson Institute.

King-Smith, D. (2008) *The Water Horse*, London: Puffin.

Munns, G., Authur, L., Downes, T. and Power, A. (2006) *Motivation and Engagement of Boys*, Australian Government Department for Education.

Northern Ireland Audit Office (2006) *Improving Literacy and Numeracy in Schools (Northern Ireland)*, Belfast: Northern Ireland Audit Office.

Ofsted (2003) *Yes He Can: Schools where boys write well*, Ofsted Publications Centre Primary National Strategy and United Kingdom Literacy Association.

Riordan, R. (2008) *Percy Jackson and the Sea Monsters*, London: Puffin.

Robson, D., Hickey, I. and Flanagan, M. (2007) 'The Leonardo Effect, Art and science working together', *START Magazine* NSEAD.

Safford, K., O'Sullivan, O. and Barrs, M. (2004) *Boys' On The Margin: Promoting boy literacy and learning at Key Stage Two*, London: Centre for Language in Primary Education.

The National Advisory Committee on Creative and Cultural Education (NACCCE) (1999) *All Our Futures: Creativity, culture and education*, London: DfEE.

13

Assessment of The Leonardo Effect Learning in Our School

Dyfrig Ellis

'*Dyro dy law i mi, ac fe awn i ben y mynydd*' – our school motto roughly translates as 'Give me your hand and together we'll reach the mountain top'. Note the inclusion of the word 'together', which is instrumental in the success of The Leonardo Effect at Ysgol Lon Las. This is what sets The Leonardo Effect apart from our conventional notion of a 'Thematic' or 'Cross-Curricular' approach to teaching and learning. The Leonardo Effect has allowed learning to be more natural and less fragmented. Our school day is no longer divided into different subject areas where pupils practise exercises related more often than not to what the teacher thinks up. Adults and children stand side by side. The teacher has become a fine-tuned facilitator and the pupils, in their endless pursuit of new ideas, have become more motivated, independent, flexible, knowledgeable learners.

Giving learners ownership over what is learnt, deciding how and when it is learnt, has allowed literacy to grow progressively. No longer do we have four different subjects every day, with four totally unrelated word banks. Learners are able to apply reading strategies in order to make connections between the text and their lives. They engage in pre-reading, reading, and post-reading strategies in order to enhance comprehension and apply evidence-based strategies to learn new vocabulary. This approach increases the effectiveness of their reading comprehension, written and oral communication as they read and analyse literary, persuasive and expository texts.

We now have guided and connected ideas synchronised effectively to allow pupils to learn and develop skills. If children do not learn the way we teach, we must teach the way they learn and start at a point of interest to them before radiating out from it like ripples from a stone thrown in the water. Like Leonardo da Vinci, children need to approach daily tasks with an arsenal of skills at their disposal and we have a duty to enrich learning, enabling them to approach these tasks both confidently and creatively.

Our experience shows that by developing a whole school thematic approach through The Leonardo Effect, learners will:

- have fun;
- be more confident and better motivated;
- present fewer discipline problems;
- be more actively involved; and
- develop learning skills more quickly as each one is connected to and reinforced by the other.

Teachers also find teaching more fun. As one member of staff told me, 'This is what teaching is all about!' Nevertheless, teachers still find teaching equally as exhausting as they plan activities based on skills development rather than knowledge acquisition that allow pupils to:

- question and challenge;
- make connections and see relationships;
- envisage what might be;
- explore ideas and keep options open; and
- reflect critically on ideas, actions and outcomes.

Our teaching has moved outside the narrow confines of the National Curriculum in Wales and planning is no longer driven by what 'needs' to be learnt. We now look at how the children learn and facilitate that learning accordingly. However, we still have a statutory requirement to provide National Curriculum Levels and Foundation Phase outcomes for each learner. It is imperative therefore that we have rigorous and embedded procedures to equip us to do this effectively. Our aim, through The Leonardo Effect, is to improve learning and achievement. Teacher assessment must therefore be accurate and constant throughout the school so that it is a true record of the school's performance and also a valuable tool to support planning.

It is still quite common to track the academic progress of pupils through primary school purely by administering standardised tests. Such tests provide teachers with levels for each child, usually for reading, writing, mathematics and science, and by comparing results year-on-year it may be possible to identify in advance which pupils are likely to reach national standards at age 11. Tests do not cover every subject of the curriculum, and being brief they do not cover any subject comprehensively. The levels they produce are quite 'broad', which can corrupt the results. With annual testing it can take a long time for a problem to be identified, and test levels alone will not identify the problem very precisely.

The Leonardo Effect has meant that teachers, through daily interaction and collaborative learning, are far better equipped to assess pupils' development more frequently and more accurately. At Lon Las we use an on-line system called Incerts. Incerts assists teachers in continuously recording skill-by-skill assessments across all National Curriculum subjects. As well as giving a level like a test, the system identifies specific strengths and weaknesses in each child's learning, and it gives this information clearly enough and early enough for teachers and school leaders to make good use of it. Assessment for the purpose of guiding teaching addresses each child's specific skills and is an important aspect of the personalised learning developed at Lon Las through The Leonardo Effect.

Our school has worked closely with Incerts (www.incerts.org) to organise the National Curriculum in Wales into sets of distinct, named skills that progress through the levels. For example, 'Writing' includes skills named Organisation and Structure, Spelling, and 'Science' includes Planning and Enquiry, Making Predictions, Fair Tests etc. Similarly, Incerts breaks down each Area of Learning of the new Foundation Phase into its constituent skills. For each skill, we have descriptions at Outcomes 4, 5 and 6 with the corresponding descriptions in Levels 1, 2 and 3 of the National Curriculum. We are now able to track a pupil's progress skill-by-skill from Foundation Phase through to KS2 in all subjects – even though we do not teach subjects in the traditional way.

As teachers record individual pupils' strengths and weaknesses, Incerts shows us which other pupils are working within the same levels. This has been invaluable for planning. The same data are also detailed enough to support report writing for parents and are a sound basis for measuring pupil progress consistently in all subjects (Figure 13.1).

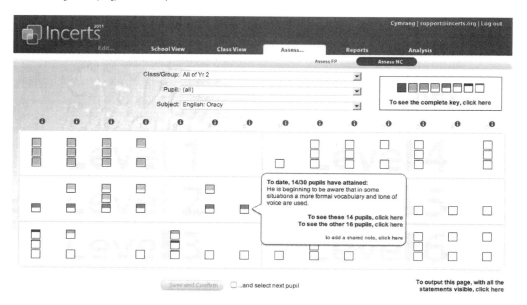

FIGURE 13.1 Screen view of Incerts online assessment as used in Ysgol Lon Las by all teachers

Teachers, learners and learners' parents are encouraged to discuss and moderate their judgements, and to take responsibility both for the assessments they make and for the progress measures and targets derived from them.

Since we now record attainment against individual skills within each subject, Incerts is able to look at several 'steps' on several 'ladders' when it calculates a pupil's level. Incerts can express a pupil's progress as a 'fine level', with a margin of error small enough to measure progress reliably year-on-year or even term-on-term. Therefore it is now possible for us to differentiate between pupils who are making some, albeit slow progress, from pupils who are making none. It is also easy to spot, within the first term, those pupils who have made an unusually slow start to the school year.

Our school curriculum has been broadly developed around the requirements of The National Curriculum in Wales (Welsh Assembly Government 2008) to include six 'themes' for every year group. These have been carefully chosen to ensure that over each 2-year period, the breadth of the curriculum is covered fully. We are mindful that we cannot eliminate any portion of the curriculum as this would compromise the learners' ability to achieve. However, the curriculum is viewed as a guideline that can be easily adapted to suit the needs of the learner. As previously stated, the use of Incerts ensures that all statutory elements of the curriculum are met. The amount of time provided for teaching the curriculum is reviewed regularly by the School Policy and Curriculum Committee and the governing body is fully involved in the decision-making processes that relate to the breadth and balance of the curriculum.

We have developed The Leonardo Effect throughout the school on the basis that pupils acquire knowledge best when learning in the context of a coherent 'whole'. We have endeavoured to put the teaching of cognitive skills in the context of the real world with a firm expectation that learning should be practical and broad enough to allow for creative exploration.

The teachers, learning assistants and pupils are all involved in setting learning objectives. The initial planning, however, requires considerable work on the part of teachers. This involves changing timetabled activities, arranging vital educational visits, teaching in teams, bringing in outside experts and enthusiasts as well as sharing resources.

Our themes are mapped over a 2-year period and show clearly what will be taught so that important links between subjects are maximised. Elements of history are studied as part of a history-based topic such as the Egyptians or the Second World War; religious topics are studied during themes on India or Bangladesh; environmental issues during themes such as 'Our World'.

Each year group plans to develop key skills through carefully orchestrated activities. The Skills Framework, Wales (Department for Children, Education, Lifelong Learning and Skills 2007) is used as a basis to plan for skill development in each subject and skills acquisition and progression within each is tracked within Incerts. Each learner will have several objectives for each task, ensuring that both subject knowledge and skills development are addressed and developed at an appropriate level. It is important that children are given plenty of opportunities to practise acquired skills so that they may transfer these skills to everyday tasks in later life.

First-hand experiences offered through regular educational visits foster curiosity and creativity, and consequently lessons are interesting, enjoyable, relevant and challenging for the learner. Their natural disposition to learn must be stimulated by everyday sensory experiences and this can only be achieved by delivering lessons in a variety of ways by providing as many first-hand practical experiences as possible.

The first steps in planning for a theme are taken by the pupils. They spend a day at the end of every half term creating a mind map or topic web to create a context for their learning during the forthcoming half term. These mind maps are usually written as questions. For example, for 'Flight' the children wanted to find answers to questions such as: 'Who was the first man to fly?', 'Why are bees yellow and black?' and so forth. The 'questions' are then collected by the teachers and carefully mapped for opportunities to develop skills. The mind map is then broken down into areas of study, one for each week. The planning will focus on up to half a dozen outcomes for half a term. These are directly linked to the key skills that are taught and developed, showing also the links between subjects. This process is extremely important because the learners have to have ownership over their learning so that they may take an active part in assessment for learning.

Teachers plan on a weekly basis, which includes detailed outlines of the main learning objectives/areas to be taught. Skills to be developed each half term are highlighted through Incerts to be certain that the breadth of teaching and learning ensures appropriate curriculum coverage. For example, during scientific activities, emphasis is placed on the teaching of scientific skills such as predicting, estimating, measuring, fair testing, hypothesising and drawing conclusions. However, these skills cannot be developed fully without considering which genres are the most appropriate to use when presenting information. Pupils should think about what they have done in order to consolidate learning and transfer skills, knowledge and understanding to other contexts.

The impact of The Leonardo Effect on teaching and learning as a powerful pedagogical strategy is an integral part our planning for school improvement. It allows teachers to take ownership of the nature, pace and direction of their teaching. It also allows teachers to make manageable but significant changes to their teaching, which usually brings an immediate response from pupils, parents and co-workers. This response from pupils and parents invites and encourages teachers to sustain the development of 'Leonardo' throughout the school. It has empowered teaching and learning in such a way that children tackle questions, solve problems and formulate ideas that are new to them without the fear of being wrong.

National Curriculum assessment results show that the majority of pupils at 7 years at the end of Key Stage 1, and at 11 years at the end of Key Stage 2, attain excellent standards. These results place Ysgol Gymrag Lon Las among the best 25 per cent in Wales during the last 3 years for pupils aged 7 years and for the last 2 years for 11-year-old pupils, when compared with schools in similar social and economic circumstances. By implementing The Leonardo Effect, pupils throughout the school develop well as independent learners. They build on prior knowledge effectively, develop appropriate strategies for solving problems and readily adapt their understanding and skills to new situations. As a result, they are able to express their opinions and views clearly and confidently. They are also able to speak appropriately and easily in formal situations when necessary. In addition, they make excellent progress in their literacy and thinking skills from the nursery to Year 6.

This approach has seen Lon Las join an elite handful of schools rated as 'Excellent' in every category by Estyn (Education and Training Inspectorate for Wales). In their report, published on 16 February 2012, the inspectors classed the learning experience and teaching as 'Excellent', while highlighting how 'teaching and learning is based upon themes that respond very effectively to the Welsh Government's 2008 curriculum for schools. These changes are very effective in enthusing pupils and in developing their skills to get the most out of their learning' (Estyn 2012).

School data over 4 years is used to compare performance with three groups – schools within the Local Authority, schools within a family of similar sized schools and finally all schools in Wales. Figure 13.2 shows how standards in Science have improved at Lon Las since the introduction of The Leonardo Effect in September 2007.

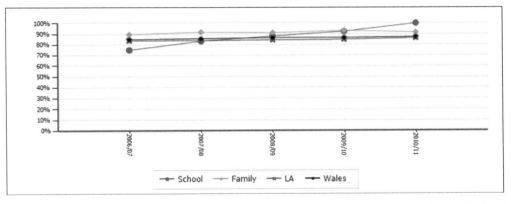

FIGURE 13.2 Graph depicting how standards in science have improved at Ysgol Lon Las, since the introduction of The Leonardo Effect in 2007 (All Wales Core Dataset, Welsh Assembly government)

If, as educators, we are to develop creative minds, we must eliminate the fear of being wrong. We have taken this principle even further by awarding children with the coverted weekly award of 'The Mistake of the Week', in a continued effort to change the way children think. How refreshing to hear a child bring his work to a teacher or classroom assistant stating 'Look Mrs Thomas, I've made a fantastic mistake!', knowing that the response will be along the lines of 'OK, let's work this one out together.' It ensures that pupils will continue to experiment confidently with their own and others' ideas. Children and staff work side by side. If a group of children are writing acrostic poems, the adult will be writing poems as well; if the more able and talented children of year 1 are learning about primary and secondary colours by mixing shades of a colour making their own shade cards, then the classroom assistant is also experimenting with what happens when you add a little bit of blue to red etc. Children see adults trying, and quite often failing at whatever task is being undertaken. But they also see the adult persevere and continue to evaluate the work, suggesting ways to improve and develop skills. The notion of reaching that mountain top together is an important one. There is a desperate need within our education system to move from wanting to know the correct answer to knowing what to do when the answer is not obvious. As Albert Einstein said, 'It is, in fact, nothing short of a miracle that the modern methods of instruction have not entirely strangled the holy curiosity of inquiry.'

References

Department for Children, Education, Lifelong Learning and Skills (2007) *Skills Framework for 3 to 19-year-olds in Wales*, Cardiff: Welsh Assembly Government. Online. Available at: http://wales.gov.uk/dcells/publications/curriculum_and_assessment/arevisedcurriculumforwales/skillsdevelopment/SKILLS_FRAMEWORK_2007_Engli1.pdf?lang=en (accessed 20 April 2012).

Estyn (2012) *Inspection information: A report on Ysgol Gynradd Gymraeg Lôn Las*. Online. Available at: http://www.estyn.gov.uk/english/provider/6702036 (accessed 10 May 2012).

Welsh Assembly Government (2008) 'National Curriculum – Key Stages 2, 3 and 4'. Online. Available at: http://wales.gov.uk/topics/educationandskills/schoolshome/curriculuminwales/arevisedcurriculumforwales/nationalcurriculum/?lang=enhttp://wales.gov.uk/topics/educationandskills/schoolshome/curriculuminwales/arevisedcurriculumforwales/nationalcurriculum/?lang=en (accessed 20 April 2012).

Conclusion

In recent years, governmental concern over standards in education has affected the way in which education is delivered in schools. The assumption that assessment of pupils is related to the assessment of schools has led increasingly to a situation where many teachers focus on assessment, particularly in the areas of literacy and numeracy, to the detriment of children's learning. The concept of 'teaching to the test' has been criticised by parliamentary committees, Ofsted and others (House of Commons, Children, Schools and Families Committee 2008; Marley 2008; Paton 2010, 2012).

We would argue that the approach to children's learning set out in the preceding chapters represents a genuine alternative, bringing together the arts and the sciences in a manner that replicates working processes used by artists and scientists, in pursuit of knowledge, understanding and innovation. It places the emphasis directly on the concepts of experiential and active learning, where children genuinely engage, develop ideas, think analytically and achieve. Teachers also have the freedom to fulfil their professional role as inspiring educators.

Does The Leonardo Effect produce tangible results in schools? The answer is an unequivocal yes. Chapter 5 deals specifically with the evidence from The Leonardo Effect national pilot, where teachers, head teachers, parents and pupils expressed their views across a wide range of areas, from subject learning to literacy attainment and development of transferable skills. The data collected by researchers is substantiated by the case studies in Part Two of the book. Here teachers and head teachers describe how The Leonardo Effect transformed learning in their schools, and this is evidenced by school inspections.

Certain common findings begin to emerge:

- how disaffected learners respond to this approach in ways that surprise even their teachers and how disciplinary problems reduce during Leonardo Effect learning;

- how schools have been able to raise attainment for both the least and most able learners and use The Leonardo Effect as a model for curriculum coherency, facilitating the demands of new curricula;

- how parental involvement has increased;

- how literacy levels are strongly enhanced by The Leonardo Effect, as described in Chapter 6 and several of the case studies.

These results are significant and verified by the fact that schools have continued to use the approach in their teaching. Our aim at all times has been to apply the synchronized integration of art and science to promote the development of confident, competent, enthusiastic children who will be capable of contributing to society and be equipped with necessary learning skills.

The Leonardo Effect is not the only method that can be used to improve children's educational attainment, but it is clear from the material described in the preceding chapters that it is one that works, and this fact is increasingly being realised, not only by the network of schools that use the methodology, but significantly also by LEAs and inspectorates. Further information can be found at www.leonardoeffect.com.

References

House of Commons Children, Schools and Families Committee (2008) *Testing and Assessment*, London: The Stationery Office.

Marley, D. (2008) 'Ofsted slams teaching to the test'. *Times Educational Supplement*. Online. Available at: http://www.tes.co.uk/article.aspx?storycode=6000653 (accessed 8 May 2012).

Paton, G. (2010) 'Sats exams promote "teaching to the test"'. *The Telegraph*. Online. Available at: http://www.telegraph.co.uk/education/educationnews/7559726/Sats-exams-promote-teaching-to-the-test.html (accessed 12 May 2012).

Paton, G. (2012) 'Heads threaten fresh boycott of primary school'. *The Telegraph*. Online. Available at: http://www.telegraph.co.uk/education/educationnews/9249146/Heads-threaten-fresh-boycott-of-primary-school-exams.html (accessed on 8 May 2012).

Appendix: Sample Format for a Scheme of Work

The Leonardo Effect *Flexible* Scheme of Work
(All categories below are intended to be expandable)

Who & When: e.g. Primary 6 – Miss Smyth – Autumn Term

Topic: (Imaginative, engaging title or question, relevant to art & science)

e.g. NOISE – SSShhhhh!!

Background: (The previous knowledge and experiences/opportunities that the children have had relevant to this work.)

Curriculum Information: e.g. school focus this term is:

General Expected Outcomes/Intentions/Objectives
(General Expected Outcomes represent the knowledge, skills, understanding and attitudes that pupils will be expected to have gained, as a result of their learning at the end of this scheme.)

Pupils should be able to: e.g. investigate the mechanics of how the ear works, play with sounds, and design experiments associated with creating sounds. (JLO Science, Art, *Music*)

ACTIVITIES	RESOURCES	EQUIPMENT/ MATERIALS
Research/Observation/ Gathering Information: (Pupils should have opportunities to: research the topic, explore, experiment, describe & discuss . . . They should be encouraged to collect visual and other information to help them explore their topic – books, cards, pictures, objects, make sketches, make	*Sound Sources:* e.g. swimming pool; echoes; the wind; bees. *Experts:* e.g. physicist; musician; doctor.	*Equipment:* e.g. dicta-phone; MP3 player; cameras; scissors; glue guns; bottles; tuning forks; burglar alarm kit; buzzers and wiring kits; cord telephones;

notes, take photographs – and use these as a resource for further work. Pupils should be provided with access to stimulating first-hand experiences. Talk, ask questions, share ideas and experiences, observe and record. Study examples of work by scientists, artists & designers.)

e.g. using a sound recorder, select and record sounds from first-hand experience and take photographs to document the sources.

Experimentation/ Developing Ideas:
(More focused exploration in response to pupils' interests. Pupils will have discussions, play with ideas, carry out experiments, build prototypes, decision make, work as teams, experiment with media. Identify actions to be taken to progress. Consider the work of artists, scientists, designers to explore different ideas, approaches and techniques and plan for the next stage.)

e.g. experiments in real contexts to grasp how sound alters with distance, through insulation, over the telephone etc.

e.g. explore and experiment with colour and symbols associated with sound by artists and scientists, to express feelings/emotions. *(Kandinsky/ Morse Code)*

Creation/Applying Knowledge:
(If appropriate, children should work towards realising their ideas by applying what has been learned in design, making and expressing. Pupils can work in teams with specific roles. Participation, engagement

Online Sources: e.g. www.youtube.com www.tate.org.uk

Artworks: e.g. 'Singing Ringing Tree' by Tonkin Liu Architects; Theo Jansen's kinetic sculptures; Susan Philipsz Sound Installations; Wassily Kandinsky's music paintings.

Music Resources: e.g. sheet music (depicting symbols); recordings of Beethoven's 'Silencio' and Rimsky-Korsakov's 'Flight of the Bumblebee'.

Books: e.g. sound by Nick Arnold

DVDs: e.g. RSPB Bird Song

Artefacts and Objects: e.g. Trumpet and/or string instruments.

Field Trips: e.g. The Orchestra, science museum.

drums with rice grains.

Materials: e.g. white and coloured paper ranging from A2 size sheets to A5; coloured marker pens; charcoal sticks; chalk pastels; large & small paint brushes; sponges; wire; tissue paper; glue.

ownership and learning are fully apparent at this stage.) e.g. make a short film involving lots of different sounds woven into a narrative (conveying pitch rhythm etc.). e.g. invent and create a musical instrument or interactive sculpture for the school. e.g. indicate parts of the work that have been particularly successful and suggest how their work could be modified or improved. **Extension** e.g. pupils present what has been created for family and friends.		
Literacy, Numeracy and Transferable Skills: (This section should indicate the opportunities pupils will have to develop their literacy, numeracy and other transferable skills.) e.g. questioning; describing; discussing; explaining; informing, using descriptive language; listening to each other; communicating ideas using subject specific language. e.g. self-management: organising, planning, seeking advice; being aware of personal strengths.		
Assessment:		
Notes:		

Compiled by D. Robson and M. Flanagan

Glossary

AfL	Assessment for Learning
ASE	Association for Science Education
BERA	British Educational Research Association
CCEA	Council for the Curriculum Examinations and Assessment
CERI	Centre for Educational Research and Innovation
CfE	Curriculum for Excellence, Scotland
CPD	Continuing Professional Development
DEIS	Delivering Equality of Opportunity to Schools
EAL	English as an Additional Language
ESCalate	Education Subject Centre Advanced Learning and Teaching in Education
Estyn	Education and Training Inspectorate for Wales
GCSE	General Certificate of Secondary Education
HMI	Her Majesty's Inspectorate of Education
HMIE	Her Majesty's Inspectorate of Education, Scotland
IDL	Interdisciplinary Learning
JLO	Joint Learning Outcome/Intention/Objective
KWL	What we know; what we want to know; what we have learned
MIT	Massachusetts Institute of Technology
NACCCE	National Advisory Committee on Creative and Cultural Education
NESTA	National Endowment for Science, Technology and the Arts
NSEAD	National Society for Education in Art and Design
OECD	Organization for Economic Cooperation and Development
OFSTED	The Office for Standards in Education, Children's Services and Skills
PCHA	The President's Committee on the Arts and the Humanities
PISA	Programme for International Student Assessment
RSPB	The Royal Society for the Protection of Birds
SESE	Social, Environmental and Scientific Education
STEAM	Science, Technology, Engineering, Art and Mathematics
STEM	Science, Technology, Engineering and Mathematics
TERU	Technology Education Research Unit
TIMSS	Trends in International Mathematics and Science Study
TLRP	Teaching and Learning Research Programme
WWT	Wildfowl & Wetlands Trust

Index

aesthetic awareness/experience 15, 16, 20, 44, 46–7, 53, 106, 129
animation 46, 54, 89, 116
arc-of-life learning 95
Ars Electronica FutureLab 43
art 3, 4, 11–21, 37, 45, 62, 102, 112, 117, 124, 131, 134, 136; abstract 16, 46; conceptual 16; devaluation of 12; display of 12; education in 11–12, 16, 20, 22; as human instinct 11; learning in/through 14–21; marginalisation of 39; nature of 13–14; and science 3–5, 21, 38, 39, 41–3, 46, 108, 118, 126; societal relevance of 43; teaching of 6, 12–14; and treats/punishment 13; visual 4, 16, 111, 133
art curriculum 15
art and design 5, 11, 14, 16, 20–1, 43, 134
art education 6, 12–17, 19–22, 38, 134; attitudes to 38
art-making, informed 37
art and science 3–5, 21, 38, 39, 41–3, 46, 108, 118, 126
art–science commonalities 21, 41, 42, 44–8, 51–3, 56, 62, 112, 116
ArtScience Labs 4, 43
art–science synchronisation 47, 74, 120
arts, the 2, 4–5, 11–12, 19–22, 25, 38–9, 42, 44, 45–6, 102, 131, 147
arts integration 21
Asperger's syndrome 128
assessment 105–6, 141–6; self- 106; of skills 7, 73–4
attainment 1, 71, 119, 143, 147; learning 5; literacy 7, 20, 41, 74, 132, 134, 138, 147–8

attention deficit hyperactivity disorder 127–8
attitude: academic 42; of children 41, 64, 136, 149; to education 25, 38, 81, 115, 116; of parents 77; of teachers 134

blindness 112–13
brain 92–5
Braque, George 46

Cambridge Primary Review, The 3, 11, 17, 22, 28, 43, 134
Catalytic Clothing 42
CERN 42, 45
child-centred approach 18
child development 6, 19, 20
citizenship education 20,94
collaborative learning 18, 20, 42, 57, 86–7, 94, 105, 111, 128–9, 142
communication skills 1, 72
Confucius 107
connected learning 38–9
constructivism 17, 28–9, 40
Continuous Professional Development 30
conversation 84, 86, 94, 95, 122, 124
creative process 14, 20
creative schools 2
creative writing 19, 136–8
creativity 2, 22, 29, 41, 45–6, 54, 70, 77, 93, 99–103, 106, 129, 133; in science 2, 28, 33; of teacher 17, 70, 105
critical thinking 16, 19, 41, 87, 99
Crookfur Primary School 115–19, 125, 129, 131
cross-curricular approach 40, 56, 112, 116, 140
cultural education 2

curiosity 18, 19, 39, 41, 42, 43, 54, 56, 69–70, 80, 83, 84, 85, 101, 106, 116, 117, 121, 127, 133, 135, 136, 144, 146
curriculum 29, 31, 38, 40, 55, 63–4, 81, 83, 85, 87, 91, 96, 102, 103, 105–6, 115, 117, 120, 124, 125, 130, 134, 147–8; creative 104; fragmented 40; integrated 53, 134; 'national' 2, 26, 141–4; in Northern Ireland 2, 3, 26, 84, 137; Public Understanding of Science 30; in Scotland 2, 7, 40, 115–19, 125, 127, 130–1; Twenty First Century Science 30–1, 33; in Wales 2, 40, 103, 105, 141–3
Curriculum for Excellence 2–3, 7, 26, 63, 115, 125, 130–1

dancing 1
Darwin, Charles 65
deaf children 108–12
Degas, Edgar 112
design 14, 25, 31, 37, 53, 64, 87, 102, 111, 123, 128, 129, 130, 137, 149–50 see also art and design
desire to learn 1
Dewey, John 40, 45
dialogue 34, 124
disaffected learners 54, 81, 147
discipline 12, 141
discovery learning 25, 34, 52, 69, 133
Drake Music Project 113
drama 12, 19, 111, 113, 116, 120, 124, 136

Edinburgh Butterfly Kingdom 130
education 100; developmental approach to 18; emotional context of 19; parental involvement in 64–5; purpose of 3, 117
education reviews 1
'educational failure' 1
Edwards, David 43
Einstein, Albert 46, 146
emotional intelligence 22
engagement 16, 17, 20, 41, 47, 73, 88, 95, 132, 134–5, 150
engineering 4, 5, 25, 37
environment, the 30, 31–2, 44, 59, 64, 99–100, 103, 127
eureka moments 4

experiential learning 40, 42, 69, 90, 104, 105, 147
experimentation 14, 17, 19, 28, 29, 31, 33, 39, 43, 44, 45, 52–3, 57, 59, 62, 84, 88, 95, 104, 116, 118, 136, 146, 148, 149–50
experts 32, 52, 54, 59, 64, 88, 102, 109, 112, 116, 119, 125, 128
explanation writing 90–2
external evaluation 6, 51, 61, 63, 66, 81

facilitators 41, 109, 117, 125, 135, 140
fields of study 39, 44
fishing, theme of 135–6
flexible planning 51, 67, 81, 135, 138
flight, theme of 53, 55, 65, 67, 70, 71, 73, 84, 86–8, 94, 95, 101, 103, 105, 108–14, 116, 121, 126–30, 144
four-stage structure 51–4, 56–7

genetics 28
geography 3, 21, 124
gifted pupils 81, 122
Glasgow Science Centre 129
globalisation 22, 38

hearing impaired children 85
high achievers 37, 74
history 3, 13, 56, 124
Hockney, David 65
hyperactivity 123

Icarus 111
ICT 34, 72, 89
imagination 1, 19, 28, 33, 44, 45–6, 52, 53, 56, 60, 64, 93, 100, 101, 106, 111, 117–18, 125, 129–31, 133–6, 138; and science education 33, 45
innovation 4–5, 43, 45, 133, 136, 147
integration 21, 31, 47 87, 115–16, 120, 134, 136; synchronised 39, 44, 61–2, 76, 83, 118, 126, 138
interdisciplinary learning/teaching 3, 21, 37, 39–41, 62, 93
internet 54, 59, 65, 71, 88, 89, 123, 135–6
interpersonal skills 53, 55, 72, 94
intuition 42, 44, 45, 46–7, 53
investigation 19, 20, 29, 31–4, 37, 62, 72, 86, 99, 101, 110, 122, 134, 136, 138

Irish Primary School Curriculum 120

joint learning outcomes/intentions/
    objectives 61–2, 112, 126–8, 149
Jordanstown School 7, 108–14

key skills 34, 102, 125, 143, 144
knowledge community 94
knowledge and understanding 3, 21, 39, 87,
    110, 111, 129, 144
Kuhn, Thomas 28

Laboratoire, Le 4, 43
language skills 20, 84, 85, 113, 122
learner autonomy 51, 62, 64
learning context 14, 18–19, 106, 119
learning difficulties 55, 123
learning environment 6, 12, 18, 34, 104–5,
    112, 132, 137
learning experience 2, 12, 14, 17, 18, 31, 32,
    38, 39, 53, 54, 56, 59, 62, 63, 70, 76,
    77, 79, 81, 86, 102, 103, 113, 115, 118,
    119, 126, 127, 137, 145
learning landscape 37, 112
learning objectives 1
learning process(es) 14, 17, 51, 53, 94, 106,
    121, 137, 138
Leonardo Effect 2–7, 37, 41, 46, 47–8,
    51–66, 83, 91, 93–6, 103–6, 112,
    115–19, 120–4, 125–31, 132–4, 138,
    140–6, 147–8; and assessment 73–4,
    142–6; children's comments on 79–80,
    93; children's responses to 54–66, 118;
    evaluation of 61, 67–81; feedback
    on 6, 67–81, 93; head teachers'
    comments on 74–6, 129; origins of 39;
    parents' responses to 76–9, 93, 101,
    123–4; pilots of 5–7, 51, 53, 60–1,
    63, 66, 67–81, 83–96, 99, 101, 108–9,
    112, 114, 115–19, 120–4, 125–31, 147;
    structure/framework of 51–4, 67, 116,
    119, 120, 149–51; teachers' comments
    on 68–74, 86, 93; teacher expectations
    of 102–3
Leonardo Project 102
Leonardo da Vinci 37, 42, 44, 45, 46, 48, 62,
    65, 78, 105, 110, 111, 120, 125, 128,
    140
lip reading 108–9

listening skills 73, 84–5, 89, 110, 122, 137
literacy 6, 7, 12, 20, 24, 30, 37, 38, 43, 53,
    73, 80, 83–4, 94–6, 121–4, 126, 130,
    131, 137, 147; artistic 38; boys'
    132–8; difficulties with 72;
    emotional 94; scientific 27, 33;
    visual 89–90
literary arts 4, 108, 130, 136
Lochwinnoch RSPB Centre 116, 119, 126

mainstream 25, 34, 120, 122, 123
management 60–1, 63, 66, 67, 74, 121, 125,
    127
mapping back 51, 63–4, 103
Massachusetts Institute of Technology 42
mathematics 14, 20, 21, 53, 75, 128
methodology 3, 5, 7, 33, 39, 48, 51, 60, 75,
    95, 99, 101, 106, 109, 116, 119, 120,
    122, 124, 125, 128, 130, 131, 134, 138,
    148
mind mapping 103, 135
model-making 113
modes of inquiry 44–5, 47, 52
Monet, Claude 112
motivation to learn 1, 7, 12, 20, 53, 54, 71,
    83, 88, 93, 102, 114, 115, 121–2, 124,
    141
multi-sensory approach 52, 56 92, 94, 136
museums 11, 53, 105, 109, 150
music 4, 19, 39, 124

National Curriculum 2, 26, 141–4
NESTA 5, 6, 67
neural pathways 93
Northern Ireland Curriculum 2, 3, 26, 84,
    137
numeracy 12, 21, 24, 30, 43, 83, 94, 102,
    131, 134, 147

observation 16, 33, 38, 39, 52, 54, 57–8, 65,
    101, 104, 106, 109, 112, 113, 116, 119,
    123, 133–7, 149

parents 6, 7, 12, 41, 54, 64–5, 67, 68, 75–8,
    80–1, 83, 88, 93, 101, 111, 118, 123–4,
    142–4, 147
particle physics 45
pedagogy 21, 25, 28, 81, 131
peer review 33

personal development 26, 65–6, 95, 111

Picasso, Pablo 46

pilot 5–7, 51, 53, 60–1, 63, 66, 67–8, 74–6, 80–1, 83–6, 88–94, 99, 101, 108–9, 112, 114, 115–19, 120–1, 123–4, 125–7, 129, 131, 147

planning 12, 13, 47, 51, 56–61, 67, 69–70, 94–5, 103, 121, 144

play, children at 1, 52, 93, 130

Popper, Karl 28

portraiture 106

print making 59, 128, 136

professional judgement/opinions 47, 55, 62, 68, 74, 80

pupil voice 2, 30, 52, 66

reading 11, 20, 52, 54, 55, 70, 73, 84, 87–9, 94, 121–2, 124, 140

reflection/reflecting 2, 14, 17, 19, 21–2, 51, 54, 63, 70, 101, 135, 137, 141

Reggio Emilia approach 17–18, 40

Renaissance, the 46

representation 44, 46, 52, 136

research skills 88, 99

resources 51, 54, 59, 62, 64–6, 68, 75, 92, 104, 106, 109, 121, 125, 128, 143, 150

retention of information 54, 71, 77, 85, 88, 127–8

Robinson, Sir Ken 2, 40, 100

role play 1, 136

scheme of work 60, 103, 109, 135, 137, 149–51

science 3, 4, 25, 37, 45, 62, 75, 112, 117, 124; and art 3–5, 21, 38, 39, 41–3, 46, 108, 118, 126, 130, 131, 134, 136; as narrative 27; as social pursuit 33, 34

science–art commonalities 21, 41, 42, 44–8, 51–3, 56, 62, 112, 116

science education 2, 6, 24–33, 71, 117; and assessment 32; and discussion 31; enjoyment of 31; and fieldwork 31–2; and imagination 33, 45; and mathematics 30

Science Gallery (Dublin) 42–3

scientific knowledge 28

scientific method 28, 33

self, sense of 17

sensory experience 14, 16, 52, 56, 69, 92, 104, 113, 114, 133, 135–6, 138, 144

sign language 108

singing 2

sketchbooks/sketchpads 52, 56, 58, 65, 106, 109, 110, 122, 123

skills 2, 3, 4, 7, 15–16, 19–21, 28, 30–2, 34, 37, 39, 41, 45, 51, 53, 54, 55, 60, 64, 68, 71, 72, 74, 77, 81, 83–5, 87–9, 92, 94, 95, 99, 101–2, 105, 111, 113, 115–19, 120, 122, 124, 125, 128, 130, 136–7, 140–6, 148, 149; communication 1, 72; literacy 11, 20, 30, 41, 53, 73, 132, 133, 135, 145, 151; thinking 2, 16, 19, 45, 53, 55, 60, 72, 87, 99, 106, 113, 145; transferable 2, 19, 41, 60, 72, 74, 81, 86, 115, 147, 151

Snow, C.P. 3–4, 43

social constructivism 17

socialisation 94, 95

special educational needs (children with) 85, 95

STEAM (science, technology, engineering, arts and mathematics) 5

STEM (science, technology, engineering and mathematics) 4–5, 25

Storey, Helen 42

study skills 88–9

SymbioticA Biological Arts 42

synchronised integration 39, 44, 61–2, 76, 83, 118, 126, 138

tactile experience 15, 20, 113, 136

'Take one Object' initiative 105–6

teacher-led learning 1, 29, 61, 109, 117, 121

teachers: inspiring 2, 147; role of 14,16–17, 24, 38, 41, 95, 103, 117, 135, 147; training of 55, 61, 67, 75, 81, 105, 109, 118, 121, 125–8

teaching 1–3, 6–7, 12–14, 17, 19–22, 24, 26–30, 32–4, 39–40, 46–7, 53, 55–6, 61–2, 64–5, 68, 70, 72, 74–5, 80–1, 83, 88–9, 91, 94, 96, 99, 103, 105, 108–9, 112, 115–16, 118–19, 120, 122, 125–7, 131, 132–5, 137–8, 140–5, 147–8

technology 4–5, 25–7, 31, 42, 43, 88, 109, 113, 131

themes 31, 40, 47, 52–7, 78, 83, 86, 95, 99,

101, 103, 105, 106, 109, 112, 130, 132,
  134–5, 143–5
thinking skills 2, 16, 19, 45, 53, 55, 60, 72,
  87, 99, 106, 113, 145
Total Communication 108
transferable skills 2, 19, 41, 60, 72, 74, 81,
  86, 115, 147, 151
transferring school 30
'two cultures' 17–18, 43

Victimless Leather 42
Victorian era 40
video camera, use of 52, 59, 89, 111, 130
Vikings 39, 56
visual culture 16

visual literacy 89–90
visualisation 44, 46–7, 52, 133, 136
visually impaired children 85, 108, 112–
vocabulary extension 73, 85, 88, 123, 140
Vygotsky, Lev 17

Welsh curriculum 2, 40, 103, 105, 141–3
whole child, educating the 1
writing frames 90, 135
writing skills 11, 142

Ynystawe Primary School 6–7, 99–107
Ysgol Lon Las 140–5

zones of proximal development 95

Printed in Great Britain
by Amazon.co.uk, Ltd.,
Marston Gate.